BARRY MANILOW

BARRY MANILOW

Kalia Lulow

BALLANTINE BOOKS • NEW YORK

Grateful acknowledgment is made to the following for permission to reprint previously published material:

Ladies' Home Journal and Stephen Rubin: excerpts from "Barry" by Stephen Rubin. Copyright © 1979 by *Ladies' Home Journal* and Stephen Rubin.

Publishing Company: excerpt from THE DIVINE BETTE MIDLER by James Spada. Copyright © 1984 by James Spada.

Library of Congress Catalog Card Number: 85-90647

ISBN 0-345-32617-2

Manufactured in the United States of America

First Edition: July 1985

front cover photo: Steve Schapiro/Gamma-Liaison
back cover photo: Jim McHugh/Sygma
Interior book design by Michaelis/Carpelis design

CONTENTS

ACKNOWLEDGMENTS

I'd like to thank everyone who shared their experiences and impressions. In particular, my thanks to Elizabeth Thiels and Jackie Campbell (in Nashville and Denver), who spent time, thought, and energy to assist me. Marilyn Abraham, my editor, deserves thanks for humor and wisdom in equal proportions. Sheila Curry, editorial assistant, was patient and meticulous. Dinah Gravel was a tireless and intelligent assistant.

—Kalia Lulow

INTRODUCTION:

2:00 A.M. PARADISE CAFE

Smoky red lights reveal a romantic cabaret. Birds of paradise and droopy palms create a lavish onstage jungle. A gleaming grand piano sits in front of a jazz ensemble.

Drifting into this mellow dreamworld, Barry Manilow begins to sing fifties'-style cool jazz songs. Miraculously the enormous Art Deco palace, Radio City Music Hall, is transformed into an intimate club.

This show is Barry's gift to himself. After years of delivering well-crafted pop tunes, he has decided to sing what he wants. He cannot be sure of how his fans will react. But any risk is worth the chance to make the music of his dreams. Tonight seems designed to erase all his

1

memories of grimy gigs in small clubs and recapture the illusions he had as a young boy in the mean streets of Brooklyn, when the smooth crooning of Mel Torme and the hot solos of the great horn player Gerry Mulligan seemed to promise a musical world filled with warm easy beauty.

The two-and-a-half-hour nonstop show at Radio City is one more major Manilow production. There are four costume changes, complex sets, and an enormous variety of backup singers and musicians. Twelve synthesizers crank out high-tech frenzy.

Barry struts, croons, jokes, and stomps through his greatest hits, thrills his audience with rock 'n' roll tunes, and seduces them with soft romantic ballads. And through it all, he displays the vulnerability and bravado that make his fans from fifteen to fifty want to take care of him. They love him for his ungainly walk and his triumphant strut. His music transforms him into an appealing, even sexy, presence. But that is standard Manilow magic.

The "Paradise Cafe" set is something new. And it is the highlight of the show. Even the critics, who have often ridiculed and insulted him, nod their heads approvingly. Reluctantly, they admit this is quality.

October 30, 1984, marked the end of an old era and the beginning of a new. Barry can now look to new horizons. The movies beckon. A larger more diverse audience awaits. And the joy these new possibilities bring him was obvious to every one of the six thousand fans that packed the house each night during his record-breaking run at New York's most revered theater. The excitement began to build the moment the box office opened. Twenty-five thousand tickets sold the first day. All forty-eight thousand tickets would have sold if they could have processed the orders fast enough. No performer, not even Frank Sinatra, Peter Allen, Menudo, Rick Springfield, had ever sold so many tickets, so quickly, at such a high price. When they were all gone, the Music Hall had taken in $1,886,850 dollars. They gave Barry a plaque to celebrate.

Ironically, however, Barry's boldest and most successful musical risk scarred his relationship with his one-and-only record label, Arista.

The "Paradise Cafe" set at Radio City Music Hall was taken from *2:00 A.M. Paradise Cafe*, his new album of eleven "saloon" songs.

"I'd gotten so tired of top-40 radio, when I was deciding what I wanted to do next I got out all of my old jazz albums," Barry explained to Stephen Holden of the *New York Times*.

Barry was overwhelmed by the quality of the old songs he heard. He wasn't sure if he could duplicate them. But when Johnny Mercer's widow, Mable, gave him some unpublished lyrics to look over, he found the inspiration. "When October Goes," with Mercer lyrics and Manilow music, is the heart of the album.

Charged up, Barry called some of his favorite collaborators, and they turned out the other ten songs in a week's time. The next step was to contact some of the country's greatest jazz musicians—the late Shelly Manne on drums, Mundell Lowe on guitar, George Duvivier on bass, and (a dream of dreams) Gerry Mulligan on sax.

Three rehearsals later they were in the studio. The final master tape was done, with no overdubs, in a continuous forty-eight-minute session. Mel Tormé and Sarah Vaughan came into the studio to lay down duets with Barry. The entire package was "in the can" for less than $90,000. That's less than it cost to record one Top-Forty single!

Once the album was done, Barry presented it to his mentor, the flamboyant and brilliant head of Arista records, Clive Davis, and the staff. Insiders report, to Barry's surprise, the label didn't want to release it. They finally agreed, but only if Barry would allow them to release another *Greatest Hits* album. Much of Arista's financial stability rests on the year-in-year-out generation of Barry's superhits. And much of Barry's career stability is built on Clive Davis's incredible instinct for choosing songs and marketing musicians. Barry agreed to the proposed compromise. But colleagues predict that when the label and the rebellious artist meet to negotiate the next contract, there will be two sides to the table.

None of this can matter much to Barry now. He is secure. He has come a long, long way . . . and in a sense returned home again.

When he was a teenager, his stepfather took him to hear Gerry Mulligan at Town Hall. "I'll never forget it as long as I live," Barry repeated over and over again in early interviews. Hearing Mulligan was one of the formative experiences of his life.

"It was," he admitted with his self-deprecating humor,

"when I discovered there was more to music than 'Lady of Spain.'" Now he and Mulligan are working together.

"Paradise Cafe." What a sweet stop on that long road from Brooklyn.

SETTING THE
STAGE

THE EARLY
YEARS:

BROOKLYN AND BEYOND

Division Avenue in the Williamsburg section of Brooklyn hasn't changed much over the last forty years. It is still cluttered with shops, long rows of small houses, and worn-out apartment buildings. Noisy traffic fills the streets. Kids are everywhere. Kids in vacant lots. Kids roaming around without much place to go; neighborhood kids who may, by and large, live most of their lives near those mean streets. The languages on the small shop signs have changed as the ethnic groups have moved in and out, but the street fights are as tough as ever. When Barry Manilow was born on June 17, 1946, to Edna Manilow and Harold Pincus, this poor area became his home. Barry remembers it as a slum. For him, despite its short distance from the glitter of Manhattan, it might as well have been on the other side of the moon.

Barry has always considered himself a street kid. His Brooklyn accent remains even today.

"I lived in the streets, my hangouts were alleys and deserted parking lots. . . . Any games we played were in the gutters. But I was not a street punk."

A shy skinny kid abandoned by his father at the age of two, living with his mom and grandparents and struggling to figure out how to protect his gentle musical spirit, Barry had a lot to deal with. "I was," he has said many times, "the kid the other children beat up on."

He did not make friends easily. But those he had were very important to him. They found their own amusements. "I wasn't very good at sports. I wasn't Mr. Popularity at school. I developed a sense of humor about myself and about life." He credits his friends with helping him deal with a tough life. Those years planted the seeds of his bold yet self-deprecating stage presence that he has turned into a million-dollar personality.

Street smarts are a valuable commodity. They can make an aggressive punk almost unbeatable, but they can also make for a very sensible and practical kid. A lot of Barry's relentless drive to the top was learned in the streets of Williamsburg—as was his practical, pragmatic ability to act in his own best interest. Common sense is what he calls it.

"You become smart on the streets of New York, common sense smart," he explained in describing his down-to-earth qualities. With no father to guide him, he depended on his grandfather, as did his twenty-year-old mother—to explain logic and practicality to him. It's those well-learned lessons which Barry has said kept him from thinking too highly of himself or getting swept away with star fever.

Don't Tell Mama

When he started grade school, his mom took a job as a secretary in a toy factory. She kept it for twenty-five years. Edna Manilow is a tough, street-smart woman herself. But she, too, must have had to learn a lot about handling the world when she was a young single mother without many alternatives or resources. Today the audacious, outspoken Edna revels in the role of Barry's greatest fan.

She is also his toughest critic. Watching Ray Charles rehearse a song for one of Barry's TV specials, she said, "He sings it much better than you do." Barry's response? "What should I do? Fire her? My own mother?"

But in public she's a billboard of pride. She practically wears a T-shirt emblazoned with the words "I'm Barry Manilow's Mother." In an often-told true story that was immortalized in Barry's TV special, she emerges as a one-woman plague on Manhattan cabdrivers. Once she gets in a cab, she asks, "Do you know Barry Manilow?" If they don't, she does what she believes any self-respecting mom would do; she gets out or "she stiffs them." Without embarrassment she was quoted in *People* magazine on her theory of child rearing. "Smack them!" she said bluntly. And if Barry were to forget a Mother's Day gift? "I better get one," she retorted, "or I'll break his head." So infamous has she become that she has even gone on to perform a cabaret act herself at a Manhattan club named, coincidentally, Don't Tell Mama. She calls her between-song patter "Manilogues."

Making Music

His mom claims she first saw musical talent in Barry at the age of two when he danced to the radio. It took him a few more years until he could find his voice, however. At age three, during a visit to Times Square with his grandfather, he had his first chance to record a song. When they stopped into a booth where you could record a song for a quarter, Barry was less than eager. With the precious quarter wasting, his grandfather finally gave up on little Barry crooning "Happy Birthday." "Grandpa's quarter was going down the drain and he panicked. In those days a quarter was gold." So Grandpa went ahead and sang it himself.

Years later Barry still remembered the event and how sad it made him. He has kept a picture of his grandfather and himself, with his eyes all red from crying, that was taken shortly after the fiasco.

By age seven, he was slightly less shy and his musical talent even more evident. His mother bought him an accordion. Pictures of him at that time show a big-eyed gamin-faced kid hidden behind a huge instrument.

"Mom wasn't really into contemporary music. What

turned my family on were horas and folk music. They plopped an accordion into my hands," Barry explained. "Lady of Spain" was their idea of a good tune.

Time and patience do have their rewards. By the time Barry turned thirteen, the music and the general situation in the Manilow household was definitely improving.

For his thirteenth birthday and bar mitzvah present, he received a piano. And equally important, he got a new father. The truck-driving Irishman Willie Murphy entered the scene.

New Horizons

Many people in Barry's family had a natural musicality. There was always a radio playing. But Willie was a true aficionado. He knew West-Coast jazz players and Broadway show songs. He brought a whole new world of music into the house. And a whole new level of stability.

The family moved from Williamsburg into the Flatbush section of Brooklyn. A hardworking blue-collar area of small homes and large families, it was the next step in Barry's expanding world. He entered high school at Eastern District High.

Where once there had been only close neighborhood ties, now there was a world of new experiences. Willie's presence changed Barry's musical life. The night he took Barry into Manhattan to hear Mulligan at Town Hall, a wonderful pattern of musical adventures began.

In addition, Barry was beginning to discover that he

could earn money playing music. He often performed at weddings and bar mitzvahs. And he began to realize he could get the recognition and attention he wanted. In school he was honored as the "best musician" for a performance of De Falla's *Ritual Fire Dance*. His new sense of the world and of music was thrilling.

Because of Willie, Barry said, "I heard music I never even imagined." Rock 'n' roll had never captured his imagination. Unlike other rock or popular musicians, he says, who can claim that hearing Chuck Berry or "Rock around the Clock" changed their lives, he was not inspired by that music. It wasn't until the Beatles came out that he showed any enthusiasm for the music of his generation.

Willie also took him to see Broadway shows like *Carousel*.

"That blew me away. Things like that were more important to me in my formative years than listening to Chuck Berry." His route to stardom may have been different from that of many of his contemporaries, but time has proven that it was a very effective road to travel.

The mention of his stepfather, the man who changed his musical life, still can make him smile. Those early musical experiences were what he returned to in *Paradise Cafe*. For that and for the respite from uncertainty that Willie gave the Manilows, Barry speaks about only him as his father.

He has referred to his biological father as "his original father." Between the ages of two and stardom he saw him just twice; once when he was eleven, and once in a semi-comic encounter in a backstage dressing room. Barry retold the story to a reporter with the same gentle self-parody that he uses so often when speaking about himself. He was, he said, standing in his dressing room with his pants down around his knees, when this guy came in the door. Barry's companion Linda Allen was with him. They both looked up, wondering who this stranger was. It wasn't until the man said, "I'm your father," that Barry remembered him. He'd seen pictures. There was nothing to do but say "Hi." Harold Pincus told him he'd done a good job that night. Barry said thanks, and they said good-bye. That was about it. Barry remembers that he didn't feel much. But his friend Linda was in tears. "I know we have the same genes," Barry said in an interview sometime later, "but I just couldn't relate to it."

Growing Pains

Family life wasn't easy. Deciding how he would shape his life was also a tough decision. The contrast between the hardworking, practical background he came from and the allure of Manhattan and music made his late teens and early twenties years of conflict for Barry.

He didn't think, consciously, about becoming a professional musician. It was not a secure enough life. You couldn't get married, have a family, and pay your bills. Life demanded a more tried-and-true route.

After high school he enrolled at City College as an advertising major. He claims he chose it because it was the first listing in the catalogue. But one suspects he knew it was a potentially glamorous and lucrative career. He tried to do what was expected of him; however, the courses didn't hold his interest. He transferred after a short while to the New York School of Music.

"When I finally made the decision to change colleges I also made the decision to make music my major career," he claimed later. Nonetheless, his life was not yet on a direct path. When money ran out several semesters short of graduation, it called for a whole new game plan.

He got married. "It was the thing to do when you come from Brooklyn and you have a girl." He got a job in the CBS mailroom. He took courses at Juilliard at night. He moved to Greenwich Village. He believed he would end up as a TV executive. He was still afraid of the idea of being a full-time musician. "I thought I should be able to support myself." Of a career in music he noted, "Somebody told me there's no paycheck on Friday! No paycheck! What do you do then?"

Some of the big changes in Barry's life worked and some didn't.

The marriage was a mistake. It lasted a year. But he'd moved into a new world. "I found I was alive. I could stay out late. Meet lots of people."

For a young man who had always thought of himself as unpopular, his talent and contact with the music and show-business world in Manhattan proved a key to finding his place in the world. He couldn't have predicted it. He, too, was surprised to discover "I could be more than married. I resented being tied down. At the end, it wasn't pleasant but at least I had the courage to know it was over."

So trying to cut the ties to the past and to his family, he moved headlong into the musical mayhem that was Greenwich Village in the late sixties.

NEXT STOP
GREENWICH
VILLAGE

Barry was twenty-one, divorced, working his way up from the mailroom at CBS, studying music, and learning how to break into the Manhattan music scene. The year was 1967. New York was electric with the most current trends in politics and popular culture. The streets of Greenwich Village, inhabited just a few years earlier by serious-minded, hard-living members of the "beat" generation, teamed with an odd mixture of ardent left-wing politicos, flower children, folk musicians, and the emerging acid rockers. All over, new life-styles were emerging. Bold college kids lived together without getting married. Homosexuals became gay. Kids from the wealthy suburbs wore Fred Braun shoes, smoked marijuana, and questioned anything and everything they had ever been told. All the turmoil and strife of big-city life seemed awash with possibility and glamour. Anyone could become anything.

In a society torn by dissent, there was a surprisingly universal feeling of joy.

Around Bleeker and MacDougal Streets, clubs such as the Night Owl, Folk City, and the Bitter End lit up the night. The sounds of The Grateful Dead, Richie Havens, Paul Butterfield, James Taylor, Laura Nyro, and Tim Buckley filled the air. Ike and Tina Turner were on the charts. Jimi Hendrix, Janis Joplin, and Jim Morrison were alive. Woodstock hadn't happened yet.

There was music to be made and money to be made in the making. That was what caught Barry. He was not particularly part of the fringes of the culture. He was still rooted in the tradition of hard work and practicality. He combined his drive and desire to make something of himself with the voracious appetite that existed for good, well-trained musicians. He was a piano player who could do the job. And what he didn't know he set out to learn.

He may not have known where he was headed, but in looking back, it seems like his instincts were brilliant.

His work at CBS took him into the mainstream. This was a real-life corporate entertainment business at work. No matter how lowly the beginning jobs were, they put him on a fast track. His mingling with freelance musicians placed him in the collective talent pool. These associations made the next four years a whirlwind of change, accomplishment, and success.

The chronology is tangled. But the main threads can be traced.

CBS—from mailroom to musical director of an Emmy-Award–winning show in three years.

Teacher and coach—from backup musician to leader of the band in three years.

Jingle writer—from piano player on a demo to major singer and writer of the early seventies' best-known commercials in six months.

House pianist—from a $125-a-night house piano player at the Continental Baths to Bette Midler's musical director in three weeks.

The boy was definitely on the move.

CBS, like any of the huge entertainment conglomerates, is a blend of impersonality and loose easygoing camaraderie. In the go-go years of the sixties when money was made and spent like it came from a Monopoly game, Barry slid in at the lowest rung on the ladder. The mailroom. Above him were floors full of people who would figure importantly in the rest of his life. Clive Davis reigned with an extravagant hand at Columbia Records. His climb and subsequent fall from power would be one of the all-time fables in the music industry. Other less dramatic personalities also roamed the building. But they would prove no less important in Barry's future.

The thing about the mailroom is that you meet people. (More people than you might if you were stuck in a more prestigious "entry-level" job in one of the departments.) And every time Barry did, something good came from it. People liked him.

He quickly parlayed his new contacts into a job with the local CBS-TV station as a film editor. It was not exactly as glamorous a job as the name implies. His task was to insert commercial clips into reruns of *Leave It to Beaver* and *My Little Margie*. But, again, he was in a position to meet people and to let them know about his musical talents.

Furthermore, he was able to move to an "editing" job on *The Late Show*. Not only did he work as a commercial-inserter, but he created an arrangement of a song called "Syncopated Clock" that ran as the show's theme.

When he wasn't at the station, he was making a reputation with other young performers and musicians. He played piano in a lot of small clubs, though the money was less than ample.

He would do arrangements for singers and back them up at auditions. He'd give lessons and coaching to others. "I was THE piano player in New York." There were no gigs, he has said, he wouldn't do. He'd play cheap, he'd play for anyone, and he'd play well.

Finally the lure of playing music full-time overwhelmed the security of a regular job. He took to the road with a singer named Jeannie Lucas. Over the course of six months they played lounges and small rooms from New York to Truckee. "The both of us put this little duo together that was the worst act going," Barry said five years later.

It is not much fun to be on the road like that even if you are getting to play every night and making money for your efforts. The lure of the road fades about the fifth time you stay in a motel room that has the same bad paintings on the wall as the one you left the night before. More time can be spent packing and unpacking than playing. It is a grind.

"I don't really like touring. One airport after another. Never knowing what the food's going to be like." In 1971 he couldn't have known that the next ten years of his life would be spent more on the road than off.

So it was back to New York and a new job at CBS. The return would mark the beginning of an avalanche of new contacts and opportunities. Linda Allen, the executive producer of the show *Callback* and a woman he had met in his mailroom and *Late Show* days helped him get a job as *Callback*'s musical director and leader of the house band.

Callback, a local show that featured aspiring performers, demanded an enormous variety of musical talents from the young arranger. Every week Barry had to turn out over a dozen musical arrangements in every conceivable style, from polka to classical, pop to opera.

Barry's job was to give the band charts (musical scores) to play from. This involves taking the performer's basic arrangements and then writing out the individual parts for each instrument in the band. If the arranger has done his job well, when all the parts are played together, they blend into one smooth musical package.

Furthermore, in the world of television, the music had to be precisely timed. The training would prove invaluable for the work to come. "I came out of [that experience] with quite a lot of knowledge," Barry said.

His work put him into the inner circle of respected working musicians. No one in the public may have known who he was, but his reputation in the business was growing. When he touched the keyboards people listened.

The *Callback* show garnered an Emmy nomination and

Barry began to get more and more work. Ed Sullivan Productions was expanding into a wide range of specials and called on Barry to handle the music. With the recognition he was getting and a growing sense of confidence, he was finally ready to cut himself loose from a regular paycheck and devote himself to the serious study of music.

"One day I staged a minor revolution. I quit my job and went back to study orchestration at Juilliard." This was an exhilarating time.

"My house [on East Twenty-seventh Street in Manhattan] was like Grand Central Station," he recalled. Students and aspiring performers flocked to him for coaching and arrangements. He helped shape their material and their shows. The piano could be heard throughout the building at all hours of the day and night.

When asked, some years later, if the neighbors had objected, he said with obvious satisfaction that when they knocked on the door he expected them to complain but instead they'd be asking him to coach them, too! New York is unique in that way: The musicians-per-square-foot ratio is unequaled anywhere but backstage at a symphony hall five minutes before a concert. Life and Barry were finding themselves in perfect harmony.

Friends and Freedom

Barry's world was expanding at an exhilarating rate. All around him he was encountering new situations, new friends, and new musical opportunities. There was not a lot of time for intense, one-on-one friendships. Having gone "freelance," he was now dependent on himself to make that once-revered "Friday paycheck" appear from somewhere week in and week out. He was growing more and more confident of his abilities as an arranger and composer. People sought him out for advice and help.

"When I was twenty-six [in 1972] I was an arranger, conductor and composer. I was going to be Nelson Riddle [the leader of the NBC orchestra]. If you told me then I'd be a singer, I'd have told you you were crazy."

Barry was a high-energy, supertalented young man who always thought of himself as a background personality. But one person who saw the full potential in him from the very first was Linda Allen. She had the kind of devoted, caring belief in him that he needed. Throughout the years to come she would become more and more important in his life.

It was through Linda that Barry got another important opportunity to test his skills as a composer. She introduced him to a producer named Bro Herrod who was trying to put together an off-Broadway revival of a nineteenth-century melodrama, *The Drunkard*. He wanted some arrangements done of old standards and was receptive to having Barry write original material as well.

The collaboration was successful, and although reviewers were not kind to the show they highlighted Barry's music as "appropriate" and "delightful."

They hadn't heard anything yet!

With Linda and a few other close friends at his side,

he forged into the freelance life. At that time Bette Midler and Melissa Manchester were making the rounds of small clubs, too. Their paths crossed at places like the Improvisation where struggling talent was "showcased" (that means—worked for free). The big city was becoming a small community of friends and colleagues. All the elements were falling in place for the next two big steps in his career. By a force all its own, his new freedom and his friends would lead him to a new source of fortune (jingles) and tempt him with the lure of the spotlight (Bette).

HE DESERVED A BREAK TODAY ... AND GOT IT!

*T*he jingles business is, for many musicians, a strange blend of hard-nosed professionalism, wealth, and a kind of obscurity. The business demands a craftsmanship that far exceeds the musical abilities of most pop music superstars. It demands discipline. It also demands the ability to ignore the fact that some people may view you as a hack.

Jingles pay fantastically well, but for many artists it remains a place to go when they have failed to make it in the public side of the music business.

For Barry it was just the opposite.

"It was something I just lucked into."

Once more his talent and his drive put him in the right place at the right time. A singer had hired Barry to help make a demo. He played the piano. The demo was headed

27

for the desk of Sid Woloshin, who with his partner Gavin had begun making a name for himself as an independent jingle house.

"We noticed the piano playing," Sid can still recall fifteen years later. The singer didn't get any work, but Barry was soon called back as a piano player.

"He was very sweet. He has good (musical) judgment and a sense of melody."

More than that, he was a perfect blend of creativity and relentless desire to work. Jingle houses are the modern Tin Pan Alley. Tough-minded professionals crank out tailored melodies evoking a wide range of emotions to fit specific formulas and timings. Jingle writers are songsmiths who pay as much attention to the clock as to the melody. Time is money, spent and earned. Barry was perfectly suited to the rules of this game.

Barry began working on jingles slowly. He would sing backup or try his hand at writing. This was the time for learning the craft and establishing contacts. It was six months after he started that he wrote and recorded his first on-air jingle . . . for Western Pennsylvania Bank. It was not exactly a national campaign, but from then on the momentum picked up.

The advertising agency and Woloshin had a new jingle all ready to record. They needed a singer for the now-famous McDonald's ad "You deserve a break today." Barry won the spot, and the King of Jingles was on his way to a lucrative new career.

"The McDonald's gig earned Manilow a lot of money and earned me the everlasting enmity of the singer I replaced," Sid Woloshin recalls.

From that spot Barry gained a lot of attention, too much attention, some say. There is still resentment over the fact that many people think Barry wrote the jingle. "My God, even my own mother thinks he wrote it!" says one of the authors. Nonetheless, it served as a vehicle for Barry.

He became the voice or writer of scores of tunes. At one time he was a participant in more than thirty commercials that were airing simultaneously.

"I found that every time a jingle is aired the singer gets paid. So I started singing for everyone." Spaghetti-O-s, Pepsi, you name it. He also wrote a famous State Farm ad "Like a good neighbor, State Farm is there," and the Band-Aid song for which he won the industry equivalent of an Oscar, the Clio.

So often did he lend his talents to products like Stridex, Dodge Charger, Kentucky Fried Chicken, and Maxwell House Coffee that after a while he stopped being able to keep track of how much money he earned.

"I hired a business manager to handle my money. I'm not good at handling it," he confessed.

Two results of the jingle madness were surprising. First, a newfound security did nothing to slow Barry down or tempt him into taking it easy. He maintained his frantic obsession with playing music. He kept making the rounds of Manhattan's small clubs as an arranger and accompanist to other singers; he coached performers and lent his skill to demos. He didn't rest on his accomplishments and thus was able to make the jingles business just another passing phase in his multifaceted career.

Second, he would, initially, be dismissed as "that jingle

writer" when it came time for him to make his move into solo pop performances. However, with his instinct for self-parody, he was able to demolish the criticisms by making his jingles the centerpiece of his early musical shows. The audiences loved the tunes and the medley he had made of them. Once again the critics missed the mark. The very qualities they lambasted him for were those his fans found lovable. Manilow does not fit into neat conventional categories.

A SURE BETTE

*1*971: Barry was scrambling ahead. Jingles were not yet bringing in the fortune they later would. Part of the time he played as the house pianist at the famous Improv on West Forty-fourth Street in Manhattan—the club that has launched so many well-known comics and singers. It was a center for new-talent showcases, and some of the best new artists came through the door.

The Improv was where Barry first saw Bette Midler. She had begun to appear regularly under the sponsorship of her new manager and the club's owner, Bud Friedman. Barry and Bette had not at this point connected in any major way, and so neither of them suspected that in the near future they would form one of the most successful teams in show business history.

Bette was just developing her musical style and her onstage persona. She had not yet embraced the campy tunes and bizarre costumes that would become her hallmark. Her comedy patter was yet to become a centerpiece of her act.

Then, the music world being a relatively small one, Barry and Bette again worked together when she auditioned for her second New York play. (She had already starred in *Fiddler on the Roof* as Tzeitel.) *Salvation*, a musical set in a revival meeting, was being recast. Bette was encouraged to try for the part of a nymphomaniac. Barry Manilow had been hired to play the piano for several of the auditioning actresses.

The hopefuls were brought in to sing for the director. Barry would vamp behind them. When it was Bette's turn, he cautioned the director, "Wait till you get a load of this girl." He knew she wasn't what they were looking for, but he believed, even then, that she might be what they should be looking for.

He was right. Bette blew the top off the auditions and secured the part. Barry went back out to hustle more backup gigs, more jingles, and more work as a piano player. It took a lot of playing to make a living. For a series of auditions he sometimes made as little as twenty dollars.

For Barry it was a time of frustration and hard work. He was overplayed and underpayed. But he was locked into the musical network, and it pulled him along in its current.

Bette was as much of a hustler as Barry. While she worked the boards nightly in the play *Salvation*, she continued to play in clubs and work on her solo act. After the theater she would race down to the Improv for a late show. She took acting and dancing lessons. She combed the thrift stores for interesting costumes. She learned more and more about the music of the forties and the fifties.

Her all-consuming drive, which she has described as "not hard, not cold; it's something I have no control over," made Bette and Barry a perfect if volatile match when they finally joined forces.

Steam Baths

By day, Barry taught and coached other musicians, backed aspiring musicians and singers at auditions, made inroads into the highly respectable world of jingles, and took gigs where he could find them. By night, he came to the Continental Baths because there was work there. He stayed because there was Bette.

The Continental Baths were a part, literally, of the subterranean world. They were in the basement of the grandest belle époque building in New York, the home of Enrico Caruso and Stravinsky, Flo Ziegfeld and Babe Ruth: the Ansonia Hotel on Broadway and Seventy-third Street.

Built in 1904 with a passionate attention to detail and ornamentation, it was, in the words of Paul Goldberger, "constructed like a well-endowed soprano." The basement was a labyrinth of corridors, small rooms, steam baths, swimming pools, and a cabaret where men in towels danced with each other and adventurous couples—

fully clad—came to listen to the latest trends in music. It was a place where new talents, outside the mainstream of taste, honed their craft. Barry came to the baths as a piano player for an auditioning singer. The singer wasn't hired, but once again, the piano player stood out.

"They were paying one hundred twenty-five dollars an hour" for backing up the entertainment on Saturday nights. "For that kind of money I would play anywhere! It meant I was freed. I didn't have to take in coaching. I could write at home."

It was a good gig. The entertainment area of the baths was a swank, glitzy room adjacent to the pool. People stood around, sat on the floor, or danced. Twenty-four hours a day there was activity. Sometimes people spent the night in the small private "rooms" off the long corridors that spread out through the basement. If it was somewhat tawdry behind closed doors, according to a former patron, the area that catered to the general public was striking and slick. It was a place entertainers could let their hair down and try outrageous new acts. There were few limits.

When Bette Midler met Barry at the Baths she had already begun to make a name for herself. The year was 1971. Neither of them could have predicted what was to come.

Bette was an old hand at wowing the steamy habitués. She had begun playing there while she was appearing in *Fiddler on the Roof* in the late sixties. The owner of the baths, Steven Ostrow, had hired her after seeing her at the Improv. He paid her fifty dollars a weekend! But it didn't stay that way.

Bette had made two appearances on the Johnny Carson show. She was becoming a national wonder and a cult phenomenon. She appeared at the Baths regularly, honing her craft and her onstage character. Her salary went up.

When Bette came in for a return engagement, she had a small loyal following but no permanent band. It made sense to use Barry. They knew each other slightly, and after all, he was there anyway. But it was not a peaceful alliance.

"It was hate at first sight. Neither of us trusted the other. It was the case of two strong egos clashing."

Two explosive personalities, each ambitious and driven, both part of and removed from the bizarre world of the baths, made an uneasy combination.

"But we knew we were good for each other," Barry explained. And like the true professionals they are, they didn't let personal opinion take precedence over artistic judgment.

The picture Barry painted of the unlikely collaboration is of the house piano player, stuck in a room full of naked men in towels with Bette onstage "looking like my mother with a fox around her neck and a turban on her head. I was rolling under the piano. I cried during the ballads and she totally knocked me for a loop.

"What Bette didn't have were arrangements, and pacing. I tried to give her a musical stamp all her own," Barry has said. He sure succeeded.

Bette became a citywide cult figure. All kinds of people made the journey into the baths to catch her act. She was a topic of conversation for the local culture vultures and press alike.

Their working relationship was finally cemented in the summer of 1971. Bette had an out-of-town engagement at Mr. Kelly's posh supper club in Chicago. When she was hired, she had insisted that the club pay Barry's airfare so he could join her. She knew then that for the serious, above-ground gigs, she needed his musical judgment and ideas.

Bette and Barry were the opening act for Mort Sahl, the satirist. They stole the show. A local musician and actor stole Bette's heart. They all returned to New York to form a permanent backup group.

With this new, solid core Bette returned to the Baths in September. Barry and Bette had forged a polished, supercharged show.

Observers at the time recall how magical it was to see Bette and Barry together onstage.

"Barry was sensational for Bette," commented the owner of Mr. Kelly's. "It was quite amazing really. She could communicate to him. . . . It was like his antennae were wrapped around hers."

But Barry was more than an onstage magician. He was also the one person who could give shape and structure to the wild Miss M without dampening her spirit or interfering with the spontaneity of the act. The engagement in September of 1971 had customers waiting around the block to get in and see the Divine Miss M.

There was still a lot of tension between Bette and Barry, however. They both came from fighting stock. Bette has said that in her family, you didn't say anything you could shout. Barry and his mom battle it out to this day. Once when Edna Manilow suggested that perhaps they shouldn't fight so much, Barry responded by saying, "Why spoil a good thing?"

Still, despite this success, Barry wasn't sure he wanted to tie his dreams to another person. Even if he didn't think of himself as a centerstage musician, he wanted attention for himself. "I wanted to leave after we put the act together," he recalled. "But Bette kept pushing me to do one more gig. I WANTED A CAREER OF MY OWN." But the pleasure of being able to get paid (not extravagantly but at least consistently) for his best ideas and skills was too much of a lure. They fought, they battled, they screamed, but the team held up.

For the Record

With all the noise and hoopla surrounding Bette, life was still a struggle. For every break there were two heartbreaks. One example was during a very prestigious job at the club in Manhattan called the Downstairs. The first part of the week, the chairs were virtually empty. "There may have been six people in the place," recalls one of the few who braved a freak tropical storm to see her. It was really totally depressing. This was an important club, and it looked like it would be a disaster. But the drive to succeed overpowered the depressing reality of the situation. Bette's response? She put an ad in a local underground sex paper. She knew how to reach her hard-core audience cultivated at the Baths. It was a matter of a few

days before the place became a celebrity-watchers paradise. Limos began double-parking outside the club, and
record-label executives began to make the trip to the Village. Among them, Barry's future mentor Clive Davis,
who thought Bette was not worth the effort to get there.
That was another major setback. His was, however, not
the last word. The sophisticated, urbane head of Atlantic
records, Ahmet Ertegun, caught her act, too. It was the
beginning of her long and happy recording career with
that label.

Road Show...at the Frog and Nightgown????

The time had come to get the act together, really together, and take it on the road. Bette was beginning to be
able to string together enough fifteen-hundred-dollar-a-
night shows to support a tour. Not a tour as she would
come to know them later on, but a let's-all-pile-in-the-
van-freeze-our-asses-off-and-drive-all-night tour: Boston,
Philly, Washington, and Raleigh, North Carolina, the home
of the Frog and Nightgown. They were visiting univers-
ities and small clubs all over the place. To do it right,
Bette and Barry knew they needed to expand the band.
The first addition was a trio of backup singers who became
the Harlettes. The trio consisted of Gale Kantor, Merle
Miller, and Melissa Manchester. The band was Barry
Manilow, Michael Federal, and Kevin Ellman—two tons
of talent all crammed together in a funny van that was

crowded with equipment, suitcases, and a thousand dreams.

"It was really some kind of miracle when you think about all those people who were on the same bus. Who could have guessed that so many stars would emerge from that little bus?" Peter Dallas, a part of the growing entourage, reflected some years later.

Clubs like the Cellar Door in Washington and Paul's Mall in Boston were part of the circuit in those days. Singers without records could still get bookings. They were squeezed in between more established but not yet superstar acts. From September 1971 to the spring of 1972 they covered a lot of territory.

During this time Ahmet Ertegun had taken Bette into the recording studio to cut her first album. It would turn into an eight-month ordeal that frayed nerves and tattered the relationship (temporarily) between Bette and Barry. While they were recording, they continued to hop around the country for gigs. Return engagements with Johnny Carson on the *Tonight Show* built her reputation. By April of 1972 Bette and company were playing the Sahara Hotel in Vegas. It was not Bette's ideal audience, but at least the reviews were continuing to be favorable.

Back in Manhattan to work on the record, the group was able to get a date at the well-known club The Bitter End. She was hot—and so was her band of not-yet renowneds. To capitalize on the local fervor, Barry and Bette rented out Carnegie Hall themselves—a big financial risk and one they did not expect to make money on.

The gamble paid off—the show sold out.

It was Bette's most glorious moment and an important chance for Barry to present himself as a featured performer. After a break between acts, a tall, lanky young man with a funny smile and a hesitant manner walked to center stage. Backed by Melissa Manchester, Barry did his stuff, sang his romantic ballads. The crowd, so devoted to Bette that they might have turned on any other act, was with him all the way.

Having Bette and Barry and Melissa all on one show was just too much power to be overlooked.

But Barry was a year away from making an effort to grab some of the center spotlight for himself on a regular basis. He was still, first and foremost, in his own mind, an arranger and conductor.

High Hopes

Bette's first album represented a real chance for Barry to get some credentials as a producer and arranger. He expected to be as much a part of the album's creation as he was of the stage show. But that was not to be, at least not until far too many people had tried for far too long to get the songs down right . . . and botched it up.

Barry told *New York* magazine that the label had asked him for his arrangements and then shown him the door. Bette, who was anxious, didn't speak up to demand his presence. Hot shots were brought in, tracks were laid down and torn up and laid down again.

By all accounts the process was the worst experience

either Barry or Bette had ever been through. No wonder the outcome disappointed Ertegun.

Any performer who is so geared to live stage shows is hard to capture on vinyl. It wasn't until the man who knew her onstage sound the best, Barry Manilow, was brought in to rerecord and fix up most of the tracks that the Divine Miss M sounded on record like she did in person. The final credits on the album divide up the producer's title between four people. But Barry had proven his value.

November 1972 *The Divine Miss M* was released. It unleashed an avalanche of success that, in the hard times that followed, almost buried everyone under its incredible pressure and power.

THE GRAND
SCHLEP

Life was getting hot. Bette and company had finally reached the tantalizing edges of the big time. The years of incredible, all-consuming hard work were beginning to pay off. It was also that critical time when even one misstep could seriously hurt a career—when a moment's relaxation, a sense that maybe, just maybe, you can take a breather, is the most dangerous impulse an artist can have. Ahead lies a mass of pressure, work, and obsession that makes anything that came before look like a piece of cake. Bette and Barry were at that point.

Throughout the next two years, Bette, her entourage, Barry, and Melissa would all fight to reach their goals. And often their goals were not compatible. The infighting, gossip, and public and private tensions escalated to a frenzy, but the professional results of the team effort were extraordinary creativity.

The artful creation of the Divine Miss M and her show reached perfection.

Barry was growing by leaps and bounds. His experiences in the studio with Bette's first album provided the credentials he craved as a record producer, in addition to his growing reputation as a jingles singer and writer. He was soon to have the chance to perform as a solo act within Bette's show. A record contract of his own was just around the corner.

But in November of 1972, with Bette's album just breaking on to the charts, all he knew was that life was getting far more complicated than he ever imagined possible.

Bette's Off and Running

With the release of the album, Bette formed a romantic and working relationship with a man known as her Svengali. He aroused deep distrust and anger in many around her—but always looked out for her best business interests. That man was Aaron Russo. He was the catalyst that made the potentially explosive mix of personalities already assembled around Bette erupt into heated conflicts.

Melissa Manchester was the first member of the group to flee. As she was an original Harlette, and by many accounts the most talented and energetic, her departure after the record's release was a blow to the whole group.

A woman named Charlotte Crossley took her place. Barry and Bette worked intensively to bring her into the show as quickly as possible. They would all assemble at Barry's Twenty-seventh Street apartment and spend hours at the piano fine-tuning the act. Aaron, who seemed to resent being excluded from any aspect of Bette's life, would constantly interrupt and harangue them. Scream, cry, rehearse, and scream some more was the daily pattern. The fighting spilled over into Bette's personal and working relationships with all around her. Yet many stuck by her, out of loyalty and love. She was, despite the unpleasant tension, a person who inspired and electrified her friends as much as she did her audience.

She and Barry may have threatened each other and thrown an occasional ashtray in each other's general direction, but they also got a lot out of working together. That held them together in the worst times.

Barry was able to capture Bette's spirit and ideas in finely crafted arrangements. His music conveyed the emotions and feelings that she wanted to get across. The artistic communication was intuitive.

There was no end to the electricity the two could generate together.

Reflecting on those times, Bette explained, "We used to fight. Mostly because I would want to rehearse for hours and hours and never pay him. I figured he got a salary and that was enough. Such bitchiness!" Yet she also recognized that he wrote arrangements that she liked, time after time.

The troupe had its last, truly last, appearance at the

Continental Baths in late November, after the album was out. Three thousand people were packed onto the floor around the pool for each show.

The baths behind them, they all leap-frogged out to LA for a stint at a prestigious club called the Troubadour. Then they zoomed back to New York for a still-infamous New Year's Eve show at the Lincoln Center Philharmonic Hall in Manhattan.

Next Bette flew to London to tape a Burt Bacharach special. For the show Barry was asked to do a new version of "Boogie Woogie Bugle Boy." Atlantic records felt the track on the album was too much a clone of the Andrews Sisters. They wanted something that had the Midler stamp.

Once again Barry was the person who could capture Bette on tape. Although the arrangement was designed to be used on a TV show, Barry approached the assignment as though it were for a record. That was what he knew how to do.

When the song aired on TV, the show used video trickery to allow Bette to appear as all three of the Andrews Sisters. The song was a major success.

Meanwhile, Aaron had finalized the first tour of '73. The props were packed, the sound and light equipment organized, and the costumes assembled. The musical arrangements were done, the travel arrangements secured. They all took a deep breath and charged out across the country.

Thirty Cities in Three Months

After the first dates in Rochester, Buffalo, Toronto, Chicago, and Detroit, the troupe headed west. The album was climbing into the Top Twenty. By the time they hit LA for a show at the Dorothy Chandler Pavilion (just four months after playing at the little Troubadour) they had no trouble selling out all 3,200 seats! The record had scored a Grammy. Royalties and salary combined to make Barry more financially secure than he had ever dreamed. Jingles spilled more money into his coffers.

All that was lacking was time to figure out what to do with his newfound affluence.

Weary, depleted, and frazzled from the grind of constantly touring, the victorious group returned home.

It was not much of a breather.

Bette's second album, *Bette Midler*, was in the offing. Barry was included from the beginning this time. He earned credits as producer, along with others, and as arranger. There was a lot less tension this time around, although between Aaron and Bette and the record label, it was still more pressure than most people would choose.

For Barry it was a pleasure. Producing was a dream come true. He had found a way to express his ideas.

"I love making records," Barry said sometime later. "I had discovered while doing Bette's albums that recording and producing was the life for me. I could just make records for the rest of my life. . . . I love hearing stuff that

I've done coming back at me over those speakers."

The confidence and ability to work in a recording studio was solid now. But he'd been on the road, playing onstage with Bette, feeling the incredible power that a performer can command. The crowds and the cheers had begun to seem desirable. So while he was settling into the role of producer, part of his drive and imagination was being taken over by the desire to take his place at center stage. "I wound up with the spotlight in my eyes," Barry has admitted.

With a funny blend of reluctance and unrecognized ambition, Barry took what little time he had during the rest in New York to make a tape himself.

The demo included the songs "Sweet Life," "I Am Your Child," and "Sweetwater Jones."

He worked with Ron Dante, former lead singer of The Archies and a fellow jingles singer. Although it had originally been intended as a showcase for Barry's songs and Ron's voice, Barry ended up doing the tracks himself.

Tape in hand, he began to make the rounds of the record business connections he had so carefully collected over the years. When he came upon Clive Davis, he made a sale.

Davis had landed on his feet after his dismissal from CBS. He headed a label called Bell Records. The shift from the big time to a smaller label had not dimmed his infallible sense of star potential. He knew he had a valuable commodity in Barry. They stormed into the studio, and by September of 1973 the first Barry Manilow album was ready for release.

COULD IT BE
MAGIC?

"Five new artists [are] to debut on Bell Records this week, these include Bette Midler's musical director, Barry Manilow."

Billboard, the music industry trade paper, announced Barry's record debut on the first week of September 1973. Along with Barry, Clive Davis had signed up his good friends Melissa Manchester and Ron Dante. The three musketeers who had been through so much together over the past few years were all riding a wave. No one knew that it would break as it did.

There was one big obstacle to Barry's success. He needed to go on tour to promote his own record. But Aaron had arranged another Grand Schlep for Bette and company—a three-million-dollar tour covering thirty-five cities in four months. Barry fought for a chance to appear onstage in a featured spot in each of Bette's shows.

The response was less than agreeable.

"There was a lot of backbiting at the time," one observer recalled. A lot of that seemed to come from Aaron. He thought that Bette was the center of the universe. He didn't want anything interfering with her rise to stardom. Bette, too, was not without her own objections to giving Barry a shot. She wasn't crazy about his songs. It didn't seem like he could blend in with the wild zaniness that was her hallmark.

"There were times," Bette admitted later, "when he was working with me, when he would bring me songs that I didn't like."

She'd snap about some lyric and say, "I can't stand that! Don't sing that!" But then the exact lyric would turn out to be a big hit.

She was not the only one surprised by Barry's appeal to women of all ages and by the popularity of his lyrics. A former colleague in the jingles business still maintains that "his success is one of the most mysterious things I've ever seen in my life."

Barry had been both a participant and an observer to the madness of the Divine Miss M. It made him feel sure he could do as well, even if he was different from her. It was time to stick up for himself.

"I told her, 'if I don't sing for me I don't play for you,'" Barry said in a *People* magazine interview in 1975.

That was a polite summary of the screaming and yelling that went on in order for Barry to get his shot. But when the dust settled, it was agreed that he could, without billing, appear at the beginning of the second act of her shows and do three songs.

The tensions in the Midler group were getting worse and worse. Not only was there bickering between Barry and Bette, and between Aaron and everyone, but Bette herself was so exhausted emotionally and physically that she was starting to snipe at those closest to her.

Gale and Merle, the remaining original Harlettes, left abruptly. The tour loomed, and Barry and Bette were forced to find instant replacements before they hit the road. There was it seemed, in those days of glory and grind, always an obstacle. But Barry was determined to move ahead, and he did so in his own way.

Barry had an ability to keep his distance. Even when there was fighting and yelling around him, there was a place where he retreated inside himself, where he knew what he wanted and where he was going. Nothing, not any amount of hysteria, could interfere with his sense of taking care of himself and doing his job. He alone was able to walk through the Midler storm and come out on top. The burnouts added up around him. Others who had joined forces with the Divine Madness of the Divine M were sleeping it off. But Barry just kept going. He had a lot bigger tasks ahead of him. Somewhere he knew it and found a way to marshal the energy so that he could pursue his dreams.

Bette's audiences were often very, very rowdy. A lot of drugs, costumes, rushing the stage, and carrying on. Not the kind of fans Barry would come to attract and not the kind of crowd that seems very inclined to listen to love ballads after they've just heard "Leader of the Pack." But armed with tux and tails and his own arrangements, he prepared to face Bette's fans.

"I was terrified," Barry explained. "It [performing] wasn't what I wanted to do at all. I wanted to work in the studio.

"I was totally convinced Bette's audience was going to kill me." Barry had visions of flying fruit and boos. That never happened. The fans responded.

When Barry took to the stage decked out in his white tails, perched on phone books to make the piano bench high enough, and shook his head in that gesture that had seemed no more than an awkward grimace a few months before, the audiences went wild.

At Denver's Red Rock Stadium, a girl bearing roses rushed the stage screaming "I love you." Barry got a standing ovation for "Could It Be Magic."

Even though he claims no one could have been more surprised than he was, the Midler entourage was truly stunned. They considered him "very vanilla."

The idea that girls would find him sexy came as a shock. No one had ever seen Barry as a guy that could make women swoon.

The First Album

Barry Manilow I was just that, a first record. Not bad, by any means, but not really captivating. As the tour went on, there was some excitement. *Billboard* listed it as number 206. It was a "bubbling under" pick. There was a chance it might break into the top 100 album chart. College stations began to pick up some songs. Airplay was heavy on small FM stations. When he appeared with Bette and had an enthusiastic audience response, local radio stations would add his songs to their playlist. But slowly it died. There was no hit.

That disappointment was manageable. After all, Clive Davis was willing to give him another chance with a second album, thinking his reputation would build. But in the dark days after Bette and he appeared at Berkeley's Community Theatre outside of San Francisco, it was pretty hard to feel good about anything.

The tour had taken them to San Antonio, Hawaii, and California during the month of September. LA they conquered. But San Fran was another matter.

Not only did the reviews wound Bette, they took stabs at Barry, too. This was the part of taking to the spotlight that he hadn't reckoned on. Luckily it would soon be offset by popular acclaim, allowing him, throughout his career, to have the last laugh on harsh critics.

"His [Barry's] opening number guaranteed instant obscurity and he went downhill from that," wrote the *Chronicle*'s reviewer John Wasserman. Song by song he demolished each of the four numbers Barry (backed by the Harlettes) had done. The last line concluded, ". . . you should wash your mouth out with Black Flag."

Barry did not yet have enough success and confidence to withstand the pain of that kind of review.

With his album floundering on the charts, the tensions

within the tour mounting, and the prospect of three and a half months of uninterrupted touring before him, Barry tried to keep his spirits up. Each time he took to the stage, there was the chance another critic would shoot him down.

The End of the Road

Aaron continued to make life backstage difficult for everyone. In his mind he was protecting Bette, but he was also isolating her. Other members of the group dropped out. Musicians had to be replaced.

Onstage the show had a grace, energy, and intimacy that captivated even the largest auditoriums. They went from one end of the country to the next, often with no break between cities. Detroit one night, St. Louis the next, a break of two days, and then on to Atlanta. Nashville, Memphis, and Cincinnati were visited in four days.

Yet all this frenzy was just a prelude to the final gig of the tour, the Palace Theatre on Broadway in New York. For Barry, too, this was a culmination. He would get to appear onstage, doing his own songs, in his hometown.

It was a record-breaking event that earned Bette a Tony, sold an unprecedented number of tickets, and set the stage for the year 1974, when it became apparent Barry's life could be magic . . . if he could just hold on.

Barry and Bette had worked to make the Palace Theatre show a full-tilt extravaganza. He had arranged a splashy Hawaiian number for the opener. The intensity built from there. The fans were totally wild. Celebrities lit up the audience with their glow. The crowds stormed the stage. Barry, who was playing the piano off to the side, found Bette hiding *underneath* it to get away from the throngs.

It was truly a wild event and a very special one for Barry, who would be doing a solo turn at the beginning of the second act.

Barry's grandparents came to see him for the first time. As he gazed out through the lights, he could see his grandfather sitting, with his hat still on, taking in the whole spectacle. But hat in hand, he joined the throngs for a standing ovation when it came time to cheer Barry. This was a moment of real vindication. His insecure, illogical, unreliable career had paid off. Those who were his source of love and support were forced to agree that he'd made a pretty good choice.

Still, all the glory was not without its tensions. Bette was at the end of her rope. She was so tired she'd begun to turn on Barry not just offstage but at the Palace as well. With a menacing look in her eye, more than once, she announced a spontaneous change in the order of the songs—a very upsetting decision in a performance situation.

Afterward they'd have a screaming battle. Finally it would smooth over, but Bette would repeat the "trick" the next night and the whole battle would erupt again.

The stories of their confrontations spread through the entertainment-industry gossip mills like wildfire. People were repeating that Barry had threatened to strangle Bette and Bette had said ugly things.

They were frayed. They would become more so in the next few months.

At last the tour was over, and they could relax and look forward to the release of the second Midler album, *Bette Midler*. Barry had high hopes for it because he wanted the producer credits to earn him respect and reputation. He was thinking of his future. He wanted to produce other people as well.

Unfortunately, there were one or two devastatingly bad reviews. It did not matter that the record was a hit. That it went gold. That the spring saw Bette earn a Grammy, a Tony, and a zillion new fans.

Bette was shattered. Her energies spent. She fled in the spring to Paris to recover. Barry was on his own. It was time to make the leap.

The March 2, 1974, *Billboard* noted that "Bell's Manilow is rehearsing for his new tour that begins in March. The singer-composer-pianist, now out from under the skirts of the Divine One will utilize 3 back up singers and a 5 piece band."

It was a low-key announcement for a year that would take Barry from one end of the country to the next, from obscurity to stardom, from backstage to center stage.

CENTER STAGE

THE DIVINE
MR. M

In 1974 Barry, his new four-man City Rhythm Band, and three backup singers took to the road to promote the sagging record sales of his first album. He forged on, beginning his first solo tour right after Bette's show at the Palace for the same reason. He knew the tour with Bette had not seemed to help his record sales, but it built a basis for a following. The exposure was vital.

For a singer who said over and over, "Being on the road is a drag," he plunged headfirst into the grind without hesitation. But inside, he must have been stunned to find himself the main attraction in a show.

He had made the demo that landed him a record contract because he couldn't stifle the urge to hear his songs on record. *He hadn't* intended for it to be *his voice*!

The three-song demo, made with partner Ron Dante, was to promote Barry's songs and Ron's singing. "Ron has a good voice but I knew the lyrics," Barry explained. "So I did the singing on a couple of demos instead of Ron. I hoped they might succeed. But I didn't want to go on tour to promote them."

Bell Records would not agree to give Barry the contract for the first album without a tour. So Barry bit the bullet. He fought for his featured spot in Bette's show because he realized, "You've got to do more than compose and record. You have to get out there and sell if you want the big brass ring."

With money from jingles pouring in, it seemed he could afford the big cut in salary. Small clubs pay badly. The cost of transporting musicians and equipment mounts up quickly. Over and over Barry dipped into his own pocket. The record company was not ready to foot the whole bill.

Early on in the tour, the feeling of optimism touched everyone involved. The rehearsals were demanding but worth the work. "I'm going to be a headliner," Barry said proudly. "That means I'm not going to have to fight the knives and forks as an opening act. I've done that. I've paid my dues."

There were more to be paid. Some towns were friendly. Some were disasters. Others were just blurs in between one stop and the next.

The group played some of the same clubs where Barry had worked with Bette. Mr. Kelly's in Chicago was a classy venue. The dynamite power of the Motown style backup singers plus the artful arrangements and the winning immediacy of Barry's personality worked well in that small supper club. Likewise the Troubadour and the Bitter End in New York were good gigs. But other small rooms such as Paul's Mall in Boston would be long remembered as "the lowest ebb of my life" by Barry.

The show, however, was developing into as polished a package as Bette's had been. Lighting, costumes, humor, and choreography were integral parts of the presentation. Barry wrote a song from his most famous jingles called "A Strange Medley." When it came time for that segment of the show, the piano lit up with tiny white lights, the audience sang along, and the infectious familiarity of the tunes often brought the house to its feet.

In the midst of all this, Clive Davis, Ron Dante, and Barry put together a second Barry Manilow album. In early November under his reorganization of Bell Records, Davis announced the album's debut on the Arista label. Initially, *Barry Manilow II* didn't generate a lot of attention. No one could have predicted how it would do. There was some indication when Barry appeared at Carnegie Hall on November 21.

This show "proved once and for all," in the words of the *Billboard* review, "that he can put on a whale of a show. His jingles are formidable indeed and his personality shone through."

But Barry still had to hit the road playing small rooms and building his audiences.

Typical of many of the small clubs across the country that Barry visited, the Exit/Inn in Nashville, Tennessee, had a nose for featuring performers who were just about to hit the big time. Billy Joel had been there two weeks before his first hit. John Hyatt played there off and on for years before he went to LA. Linda Ronstadt, Jimmy Buffett, and Ry Cooder had all played there. Some of the biggest names in jazz, rock, and popular music had sauntered through the entrance at the back of the one-story shoe box.

The performance room was filled with tables and chairs. Patrons were usually attentive, and the sound system was good. The dressing room was in a funny converted garage up an incline behind the kitchen.

The club owners had been "rushed by a whole slew of folks." Local people, Arista, ASCAP had all urged them to book Barry. He was scheduled to play four shows: two on Friday and two on Saturday night.

The first show was not sold out, the second a little better, but by Saturday the word had spread through that country-music capital that Barry Manilow was a "must-see" act. He electrified the audiences with the seamless, high-energy set.

"He's got everything down pat," wrote Eve Zibart, then a reviewer for the *Tennessean*. No matter that his white suit and pink-sequined T-shirt reminded her of "The Man from Glad," she found him to be "a musical hotshot in the arm. The pro turned professional . . . he's the kind of entertainer you wished," she concluded, "that they'd saved the cliches for."

There was time for the backup singers, who were earning their new name, Lady Flash, to take center stage once in a while and for Barry to deliver his now—well-known quips.

"Most love songs," he explained, "are about how 'if you'll only come back to me I'll give you my heart, my soul and my kidneys and liver. . . .'"

And he launched into "Mandy." It was not like most love songs at all. It was a superhit. By the time he left Nashville, the album hit the charts at 160 with a bullet. All the groundwork may have paid off. With fire dancing at his heels, he hit the road again. Barry found himself in Los Angeles in the early part of 1975.

Stranded actually.

Flat broke.

In despair but resigned, he had the attitude, "That's okay. I like being broke. I'm afraid of what money might do. I might relax too much. Poverty makes me struggle."

Honoring their commitments to gigs in the West, Barry found the means to get the show on the road. They had to work even if it only increased the financial strain.

Ebbet's Field in Denver, like the Exit/Inn in Nashville, prided itself on its reputation for good music and for treating its musicians well. But any gig can go wrong. And considering the strains, it's surprising something didn't go a lot "wronger."

The room was an amphitheater-style area with carpeted "bleachers" rising up all around a center stage. The stage itself was raised about four inches off the ground. It proved to be four inches too many.

Barry, with thoughts on other things, twisted his ankle very badly in rehearsal. Collapsing in pain, he was rushed to several doctors by the distraught staff. Over and over the word was "you tore a ligament. It must be put in a cast."

Barry in a cast? Onstage, playing, singing, dancing, clowning around? How was that going to work?

His personal manager called and threatened to pull him out of the club. His band, who would over and over again prove to be a source of warmth, support, and devotion, came up with their own solution. When Barry arrived for a sound check, he found everyone in his own "cast," prancing around with white gauze on one leg. Lady Flash was Lady Limp. It helped break the ice if not mend the foot!

So the show must go on, and go on it did. No matter that between every set Barry threatened to walk (or hop) out. No matter that the club insisted he honor his contract and perform, while his manager insisted his injury was the club's fault and Barry was not obligated to honor his contract. Each night, when the time came for the house lights to dim, Barry always appeared.

"He gave it his all. Onstage he was fantastic," says one of the people who had to deal with the behind-the-scenes traumas.

This was a time when the glimmer of success clashed dramatically with the fears of failure and the pressures to keep the act together. Barry, who was always effected by the hardships of his youth, must have found it hard sometimes to face an audience. He was not yet as secure and confident as he would become. He still felt like the kid who got beat up on in the old Brooklyn neighborhood.

At Fresno State, a small college in California, he was overtaken by these fears.

"I just knew the kids in the audience would be all those

kids I grew up with. . . . This was the youngest house on the tour. I just knew they were going to hate me. They're going to laugh at me and scream. I was really scared."

But he told the band, and once again they pulled him out of his despair. The three backup singers helped him through, and of course, the show was a success.

The road had, once again, exacted its tremendous toll. But this time it would pay back what it had taken. For just as Barry was at the lowest point in years, "Mandy" rocketed to number one!

In six weeks his entire life changed once again.

MANDY

1975.

Ｗith "Mandy" Barry went from Maniwho? to Manalive! He sold 4,000,000 singles, 1,600,000 *Barry Manilow II* albums. "Mandy" pulled the second album into double platinum—and then went on to spur the sale of the first album so it, too, ended up platinum.

There was some nostalgia for the old days when there was "a little less pressure, a little more freedom. It was a little more innocent."

Then "it wasn't the end of the world, every decision wasn't going to affect me for the rest of my life."

But there was little time for reflection. The demands of sustaining the success that "Mandy" promised made it necessary to tour constantly.

"Where are these fans coming from?" Barry asked in shock as they lined up around the block to catch him in

Detroit. "How," he wondered, "do they know I'm any good?"

But they'd heard through the great music grapevine. And they lined up not just in Detroit but across the country.

At Illinois State several hundred fans waited for over an hour for a chance to see Barry after his show was over. He had starshine, and the crowds responded.

By March he was returning to Nashville not to play the small Exit/Inn where he'd been in November but the huge coliseum, the War Memorial.

The pressure seemed enormous to him. The success of "Mandy" demanded that he top his million-dollar product every time he faced an audience.

"I was scared stiff. How was I supposed to follow that?" he asked *TV Guide*'s Don Kowet in an interview.

It would be a couple of years before the superstar had time to digest what was happening and begin to understand that the audiences were not asking for wild Roman spectacles. They wanted the man, the person. That was his charm and his power. But until he was able to understand the strength of his musical and personal presence, it would be hard to believe the magic would sustain.

The way you manage fame, "depends," Barry has claimed, "on what you want, it all depends on the way you're made up."

Barry was made up of tough stuff. What he wanted was not a flash in the pan but a sustaining career. Each choice he and Clive Davis and Ron Dante made was designed to ensure that. They knew that when you sell the personality, not just a trendy tune, ". . . that's the best kind of career you can ask for. When you're not reliant on how high up the charts your record goes."

It was almost as if that attitude assured Barry of having chart-climbing singles every time he crooned a song. The audiences were tripping over each other to share the wonder, the enthusiasm, and the joy that he felt at having the opportunity to communicate with so many people.

"They've seen me go through a lot of stuff onstage and they appreciate it." Barry knows they share his feelings with him and that this means his career will last "longer than a 3 minute and 45 second record."

Throughout the year the pressures and the pleasure of the road were building. But they were all worth it. It gave Barry the chance to return to the studio. He coproduced his third album, *Tryin' to Get the Feeling*, with Ron Dante.

THE AVALANCHE

*T*he next three years, from 1976 to 1979, whirled by in a blur of acclaim, record sessions, more acclaim, touring, more acclaim, and endless bouts of exhilaration and exhaustion. There was little time for a personal life, yet those closest to Barry stood by him with understanding and patience. He was as hard on others as he was on himself, and yet they marveled at his drive and talent.

That doesn't mean it was easy on the people around him. It even took its toll on Barry. But in moments of reflection and quiet, he found ways to make amends.

In 1978 he wrote a song, "Linda," with collaborator Enoch Anderson that seemed to capture the depth of his feelings and his dilemma.

Pouring out his feelings into a song proved the surest

way to communicate his awareness of the trouble he had managing relationships. By acknowledging how she "loved him back to life, but he hardly seemed to see her there," he tried to express the one set of feelings he hadn't articulated loudly enough. Linda Allen and he had shared almost a decade of hardship and glory, yet he seemed to be saying that he hardly had a second in his frantic schedule to acknowledge it.

The machinery of his career kept grinding along. He started a round of touring that left him breathless.

The ninety-eight city tour that began in August, 1976, ran through April of 1977. In the midst of that he found time to play the Tony-winning date at the Uris Theatre in December and to get his first TV special ready for airing in the spring of '77. He released the *Barry Manilow Live* album from the Uris gig, had his fourth album, *This One's for You*, go platinum, and gathered hit singles—"Weekend in New England," "Looks like We Made It," "I Write the Songs." The new album (*This One's for You*) had been on the charts for twenty-one weeks by January 1977. By February it had sold 1,500,000 copies! And...yes, he even appeared in the Macy's Thanksgiving Day Parade in New York City.

Barry also made his first inroads into the profitable world of Las Vegas and Tahoe in 1977. His first date at the Sahara Casino in State Line, Nevada, proved he could produce a solid piece of entertainment in the most competitive and commercial of environments.

At that time his tour was not as much of an equipment-toting extravaganza as it would become. He came into town backed only by his own rhythm section and Lady

Flash. The casino provided a twenty-five-piece backup orchestra.

He arranged, as he had done so many times since, for a local chorus to join him. He picked Saint Teresa's choir from a local Catholic school.

With Billy Crystal opening for him, he packed the seventeen-hundred-seat house for two shows a night. At eight he played to the dinner crowd. At midnight he entertained a house of late-night listeners. His mom came out to Nevada to see the show.

The professionalism of so "young" a performer impressed the crew and management. But when he returned in 1980 for his second date, some people noticed a change. The act had gotten "too efficient." The rehearsals were closed even to the Casino's stagehands.

"It could be the people around him," commented one casino worker who wishes to remain anonymous. He recalled that Howard Cosell was there and wanted to say hi to Barry. He refused, or at least his "people" said "Barry doesn't do that." He also refused to pose for a picture for the casino staff.

This is not the first or the last time that the people employed by a superstar damaged the "image." In their zeal to protect and assist their boss they often alienate people. Barry is aware of that and has commented on the problem.

"Now and again I'll blow up at my assistant when he thinks he's representing me and he'll yell at a waiter. How dare you? I'll say. Please don't talk to people like that. What's the matter with you?"

But Barry knows he can't be everywhere at once. He

must trust the judgments of those around him, even though they, too, occasionally succumb to pressures. As a result, despite the best efforts of everyone concerned, a reputation gets damaged. Goodwill is compromised

From Arizona to Arkansas, from Michigan to Maryland, the tour sped along. Barry lost some, won some, weathered the standard barbs of reviewers, and sold more records than anyone around.

It's enough to make anyone a little philosophic.

"I'm not a fighter," Barry claims, but when "I feel like I'm being left out of a decision, I start screaming."

One classic example was at a concert in Philadelphia, after too many cities and too few rests. A TV crew had arranged to tape three songs. Only three songs. When they continued taping after that agreed-on limit, it punched Barry's buttons.

By his own admission, he acted like a wild man. He yelled, he screamed, he even threw one of the crew against a wall. In front of him were twenty thousand fans yelling and screaming; onstage was Barry, feeding into their energy trip and getting taken over by his own. And in the wings the unfortunate crew of the TV show stood helplessly by.

It was by all accounts a classic show-business scene.

Afterward Barry said, without guile, "I had no right to scream like that." But when he performs, he is in a supercharged world all its own, and no one should step into that current without being prepared for a big shock.

"It took a lot of aspirin to get this far," Barry said in the spring of '77. His longtime professional association

with his friend, jingles singing partner, and coproducer
Ron Dante had ended. Ron wanted to try his own adventures. While his recording career would never again
match the success of the Archies, he went on to produce
Broadway shows and keep active behind the scenes. This
change was certainly a turning point. Barry has always
depended on the close support and collaboration of friends.
Dante's departure would mark a new era.

His agent and good friend Miles Lourie took out a full-
page ad in *Billboard* proclaiming the end of the tour.

Congratulations Barry—
It's been a miracle.
9 months on tour—sold out!
TV special—highest ratings for a new artist.
Record sales—4 gold LP's on charts at once
2 double platinum!
Attendance records broken all over—
Vegas, Tahoe, Ravinia, Philly, Toledo etc!
B'way sold out both weeks.
Awards up the gazoo!
Boy, do you need a vacation!
      This one's for you!

Time to retreat to the pleasures of Linda, his pet beagle, Bagel, and his glorious new digs on both coasts. In
New York he rented a larger, old-style, elegant apartment,
filled it with pinball games and recording equipment, and
prepared to relax. In California he contemplated a posh
mansion in the canyons—"for tax reasons."

He'd accumulated enough top singles in the last two and a half years to put together his first *Greatest Hits* album. It was another record breaker.

To take it easy, he devoted four months of relentless work to the production of his second TV special for ABC and to recording *Even Now*, which featured the Grammy-Award-winning single "Copacabana" and the hit "I Can't Smile without You."

That's taking it easy?

I NEED YOUR
HELP, BARRY
MANILOW

*B*arry had made it to the big time. Ray Stevens, a Nashville songwriter and studio owner, cut a single making fun of the romantic Manilow ballads. He called it "I Need Your Help, Barry Manilow."

"Hey," Barry commented. "The album was a song of love. We both laughed about the album. When I heard it I sent him a telegram."

Barry gave his help to Dionne Warwick as well. Clive Davis signed her to an Arista contract and brought in Barry to produce the album. He was back in the studio and back in heaven. After all that time in the spotlight, he could still say, "I just love that job."

Dionne did achieve two big hits from the album, although not with any of Barry's material.

But 1979 was fulfilling for other reasons as well. Barry

won his Grammy for "Copacabana." It is the seal of approval of the music industry. Looking shy in his crisp black tuxedo, Barry accepted the award with an expression of awe.

His third TV special aired in the spring after another grueling four-month ordeal of putting it together. When it was over, it was time to head for Palm Springs.

There amid the cactus and swimming pools, Barry spent three months getting *One Voice* in form for a fall release.

From the thirty-two songs he had penned in the recent months, he culled the best. Combining them with Clive Davis's golden picks, he ended up with two hits, "Ships" and "When I Wanted You." The album itself went double platinum!

The release of another album of course necessitates another extended tour, but Barry felt he had to save his energy for a major push in 1981.

Instead, he opted for a less hectic and shorter schedule. But even a limited Manilow tour is a big deal. Every city he visited had to be treated to the Manilow magic. He launched massive productions complete with the UNICEF choir. By now he had a large road crew assembled that worked as advance men, staying one jump ahead of Barry as he zipped from town to town. Tons of sound and lighting equipment, a portable stage, and a tremendous number of costumes can all add up to making a short tour a major effort.

Small Is Beautiful

Grasping for a solution to the problems of staging one large production after another, Barry decided to try a whole new approach.

Why not play small clubs? Why not experiment with new material? Why not do it without publicity? Why not have fun?

These "open rehearsal" performances, as he called them, provided him with a unique chance to express himself.

"I do an entire evening without going back to any of the songs that have been real famous," he explained at the time.

"I still got three standing ovations in New York so now I'll be able to do the old stuff on the [upcoming] tour without thinking they're just applauding for the old stuff."

Barry was expressing a hidden, if common, apprehension that plagues many established stars. They don't want to become their own museum exhibit of oldies but goodies. They don't want to be loved only for what is past. They want to know that the fans respond to them, at the moment, as they are changing. The mini–sneak tour gave Barry a chance to test his appeal divorced from the hype of the record company and the nostalgia of the fans. It proved a tremendous success and a relief.

He described the *musica operendi* as follows: "We sneak into a city without any advertising at all. We leak it to the

press a day before so some people will show up. The
tickets are $5 each. There's no VIP list, no secretaries of
record companies getting in for nothing, no reviewers."

It was just Barry, his musical ideas, and the audience.

At the same time that Barry was gaining confidence
and enjoying the fun of playing in small clubs, he began
taking acting lessons in Los Angeles with Nina Foch and
went into analysis.

Years earlier he had tried therapy, which he described
as screaming and pounding a pillow. Then he decided the
release he experienced from performing was much more
helpful than beating feathers in a small private room.

But now he found both acting and therapy were helpful.
"I feel like my feet are on the ground. Before there were
just too many moments when I was just unsure."

The acting lessons, the therapy, and the tour of small
personal clubs all worked to prepare Barry for—you
guessed it—his next tour!

"In the Round"

Barry's next round of touring was done in the round.
"Once you try it, nothing compares." To be surrounded
on all sides by fans is a feeling that is unique. From Vegas
to Denver to Madison Square Garden, he toted his massive stage, redesigning each auditorium to fit his show.

This venture was a first for another reason as well. It
took Barry and crew to Europe.

"It's going to be like playing on Mars," he said. Visiting

Germany, England, and France, where his songs had consistently topped the charts, was a whole new experience.
There, where at least a good part of the audience could
not understand the words, Barry was relying on his vibes,
the warmth of his smile, and the quirkiness of his humor
to communicate the emotions and texture of his songs.

From Paris to London to Frankfurt, Barry and his
twenty-piece orchestra, choir of voices, Flashy Ladies,
and consummate rhythm section sold out the concert halls.
If I Should Love Again, his tenth album, was released in
August. Another chart topper, this one was produced totally by Barry. It reflected his taste and touch completely.
The romantic feeling permeated every track.

This album was followed by the release of his second
Greatest Hits album. But instead of simply threading his
old standards together, he dropped in a couple of innovative tunes. He fashioned a duet with country singer
Ronnie Milsap. "Put a Quarter in the Jukebox" was a hit
on pop and country charts. The ironic thing was that Barry
and Ronnie never met!

They each laid the tracks down over the music in sep-
arate cities at different times. So busy was Barry's schedule that even a duet had to be done long distance.

The other surprises on the album were "Read 'Em and
Weep" and "You're Looking Hot Tonight."

"Read 'Em and Weep" became the track to Barry's
first rock video. Calling on Bob Giraldi, who master-
minded Michael Jackson's hit videos, Barry and crew put
together a fantasy that had him dancing and acting as a
brokenhearted clown/minstrel. Spending over seventeen

hours taping, they culled the tape to a tight three minutes.

Because Barry is not on the playlists of MTV and other more rock-oriented video stations, this marked a turning point in video production. He was saying to the programmers across the country, "Hey, there is a vast market out there for my kind of songs and my kind of singing! Pay attention!"

The current developments in video have proved him right. With MTV planning to offer more and more "Middle of the Road" (MOR) tunes on tape, many other artists with appeal to "older" audiences are following Barry. The guy can sure set a trend, even when all the doomsayers predict failure!

The six-month In the Round tour reached its peak with a concert in January of 1982 at London's Royal Albert Hall. Over half a million people lined up to try to buy the 21,500 tickets that were available.

Manilow Mania, screamed the headline of the sensational London paper the *Daily Mail*. Other papers followed suit.

Barry's entrance into England had required three hundred British bobbies to protect him from the fifteen hundred screaming fans who weathered record cold at Heathrow Airport to see their star arrive.

Not since the Beatles had caused mass hysteria among England's young had London seen such a spectacle.

The concerts at Albert Hall became the basis for *Barry Live in Britain*. That album rocketed to number one in England the first week of its release! This was a feat never before achieved by an American performer.

By spring of '82 he had three albums in a row go platinum in England. Not even the Beatles had done that in any one year!

No matter where Barry went in the States or on the Continent, the results were the same!

By spring of '82 it was time to regroup the forces and settle in for the next round of recording and touring. This was a time when Barry, confidence ever growing, decided to take one more risk. He recorded an Extended Play disc of up-tempo rock 'n' roll songs. Its release in late '82 came midway in his next massive tour. The reaction of his fans was startling!

"For the first time in my career I got hate mail from my fans when I recorded 'Oh Julie!' My fans have always been supportive in a quiet sort of way. It really surprised me!"

But they felt betrayed. Over and over they wrote asking if he was going to abandon them, going to record songs just like everyone else?

"Oh, Julie," an up-tempo rockabilly tune by Shakin' Stevens was something that Barry loved. "It was one of these songs that's so simple it's great. I can't write stuff like that," he explained. "I always try to add something and end up making it too complicated to work."

The controversy over his latest release did nothing to dim the ardor of the fans in this country or around the globe. In October of 1982 he embarked on his grandest, most "produced" tour ever. Barry's fans embraced him.

AROUND THE
WORLD IN
EIGHTY DATES

*L*oading up his private jet, outfitted to make the globe hopping as comfortable as possible, Barry packed up a revolving stage that weighed five tons and took half a dozen men to assemble and operate. All the dancing girls' costumes, the orchestra players, the lighting and sound equipment, and thirty backup singers had to be in place for each stop. The *career* had blossomed into a portable city filled with sets and personnel. There were people whom Barry barely knew, and there were friends and family who provided constant touchstones with what he longingly has called normal life.

That pull to make contact with the "real," to reach out and interact one-on-one with fans and friends, is seen clearly in the touching story of his encounter midtour with a twelve-year-old boy in the small university town of

Champaign-Urbana in the heart of Illinois.

The afternoon before the show, in order to get a bit of fresh air and see the sights, Barry and his friends piled into their stretch limo and headed for a small park. Nearby, Albert King and his sisters were playing.

"I recognized him," Albert said later, "but I wasn't going to run up to him and embarrass myself in case it wasn't him."

Finally, with the prodding of his sisters, he walked over to the star.

The young boy bubbled, "Come over and meet my mom."

And Barry did. The kids all piled into the limo with Barry and drove over to the King house.

"Oh, my God!" said Albert's mom, Diane, when it registered who was standing a few feet from her.

Barry and friends stayed for about twenty minutes and gave the Kings twelve tickets for the concert. After the show, Barry had Albert come backstage. They exchanged addresses so they could write to each other.

Those are the moments when the pleasures of being a star are vivid: it lets you make other people happy; it lets you meet new folks.

That Manilow touch is at the core of his magic. And that magic followed him across the country.

By the time he reached Murfreesboro, Tennessee, in December of '82, he had settled into a warm, smooth pace that electrified the audience. He had been on the Around the World tour for three months!

Appearing at Middle Tennessee State University he

enchanted 9,500 hundred fans with his show. Not only did he bring the forty-member university choir onstage for the last few songs, he did his patented duet with an audience member. Pat Pater was brought up to sing "I Can't Smile without You." "Despite his nose, he's gorgeous," she gushed afterward. "He has the most beautiful blue eyes."

As a local reviewer put it, "Barry Manilow is worth waiting for!" He was offering his fans the old standards and adding to them. He had brought along a whole new set of musical equipment that changed his sound radically. No more reliance on twenty-five-piece orchestras for all his arrangements. He began experimenting with electronic keyboards and synthesizers that he dubbed "dream machines." He used these new technological instruments to perform up-tempo, contemporary rock songs like "Oh, Julie."

This tour, which began in England in August of 1982, was one of the hardest treks Barry had ever undertaken. With the record industry suffering from a recession that saw even the biggest pop stars canceling dates and losing money, Barry was "Ready to Take a Chance Again."

"Don't think I'm not nervous," he said as he took to the road.

Before heading for England on the first leg of the tour, he sublet his Central Park West apartment in Manhattan to Raquel Welch and her husband. That would prove to be an arrangement that caused a lot of trouble down the road. But it seemed a perfect solution at the time. Raquel was appearing on Broadway and needed a home. Barry

was not going to be in town. However, later, when he
wanted it back, the tenants would protest their attempted
"eviction" and end up wrangling it out between lawyers
and agents.

The tour, which toted up ninety-five sold-out shows
and established thirty attendance records, started at the
magnificent Blenheim Palace just outside of London.

A two-hundred-room 450-year-old palace, originally
built by the First Duke of Marlborough, served as a
dreamlike backdrop to an outdoor concert for 40,000 Manilow maniacs. For two hours and twenty minutes, Barry
sang and joked with the devoted fans.

It was, in Barry's words, "One of the most exciting
nights" of his life.

As the sun set over the soft green fields of England,
Barry stormed the stage in front of two enormous video
screens filled with images of his profile.

Even the normally reserved eleventh duke of Marlborough conceded that the music and the fans were both
enjoyable. The shrieks of the mostly female crowd did
cut through the night air, but no sleeping noblemen or
grazing livestock seemed to object. The whole show, complete with Barry's self-parody and particularly blatant
sexual innuendoes, ended at a fevered pitch with the encore song "Hot Tonight."

At one point Barry rewarded a girl who sang with him
by giving her a T-shirt that said I Sang with Barry Manilow.

Barry's glib quip? "I've got T-shirts that say I did a lot
of other things with Barry Manilow, too."

**BARRY
MANILOW**

Above: Barry with friends Cindy Williams and Penny Marshall in front of the Carnegie Deli after a party at Xenon for Rod Stewart.

Left: Eydie Gorme congratulates Barry after another record-breaking show.

ROY EVERSON/TRANSWORLD FEATURE SYNDICATE/GLOBE PHOTOS

Top Left: Barry and Bette Midler at the opening of *Yentl.*

Lower Left: Two New York City boys who made it big share the limelight. "How'm I doin'?" asked Mayor Ed Koch.

*T*op: Dick Clark and Barry help Clive Davis celebrate the success of Arista Records at a birthday bash for the label.

*R*ight: Barry and Melissa Manchester have a lot to smile about since their early days together as jingles singers and members of Bette's show. Here they enjoy the opening-night party after Barry's 1976 Uris Theater show.

Left: Barry and his biggest fan, Edna "Mom" Manilow.

Below: Barry parties with Morgan Fairchild, Pia Zadora, and George Benson at the Red Parrot, where an opening-night fête honored his 1983 Uris Theater show.

*F*ar Right Top: Barry wows 40,000 fans at his concert at Blenheim Palace near London.
Bottom: The Flashy Ladies bop with Barry during the rock 'n' roll section of the show.

*R*ight: Barry gives it his all on the last gig of his seven-month tour in London in 1983.

*B*ottom: Radio City Music Hall, October 1984, a very special record-breaking concert.

GARY GERSHOFF/RETNA LTD.

SL/RETNA LTD.

Right: Barry receives a Grammy in 1979 for the song Copacabana. Lower Right: After he sets the Guinness Book of World Records all-time high Broadway ticket sales mark in 1983, Barry's party at the Red Parrot includes a mock-up of his backstage dressing room.

Lower Left: In 1984, Radio City Music Hall presents Barry with a plaque to commemorate his ticket sales—over $1,800,000.

Upper Left: It's official! Barry's star is planted in the Hollywood walk of stars in 1980.

JOHN T. BARR/GAMMA-LIAISON

J. BARRETT/GLOBE PHOTOS

VARIETY
BARRY BIG B'WAY BIZ

SOL

STEVE SCHAPIRO/GAMMA-LIAISON

RADECK/GAMMA-LIAISON

*F*ar left: In his quiet moments Barry can gaze at "his" stars from the patio of his Bel Air, California, home.

*T*op right: Surrounded by recording equipment and instruments, Barry spends off-hours composing.

*B*ottom right: In his private plane on tour Barry amuses himself with crossword puzzles and funny glasses.

STEVE SCHAPIRO/GAMMA-LIAISON

S. SCHAPIRO/SYGMA

Top: Reading over a script for a TV show with Goldie Hawn, Barry and his beagle, Bagle, seem undisturbed by the sign on the wall. It reads: "Old musicians never die, they just decompose."

Bottom: Barry jumps into mixing his albums with both feet.

Top: Barry with Linda Allen, whom he first met when he worked in the mailroom at CBS.

Bottom: Even in his dressing room at home Barry has to answer phone calls and fan mail.

Left: "Lady of Spain"? The accordion was the first instrument Barry ever played.

Below: Barry loves to play to a hometown crowd.

ROBIN PLATZER, IMAGES

ROBIN PLATZER, IMAGES

Top: Even if they are a handful sometimes, the Flashy Ladies make life on the road a lot more fun.

Audiences at the Apollo Theater in Manchester, England, wave thousands of electric "candles" throughout Barry's 1983 show.

*B*arry pulls out all the stops for the tune Copacabana. Under the ruffled shirt is a fake "rug" of chest hair. He once said if he sees clothes he likes in the pages of GQ, it's too late! This get-up is his alone!

One fan commented, "Barry's changed since I saw him last year." But she added she'd take him any way, any time.

Back in the States later in the tour, Barry returned to LA to make a surprise appearance onstage with Bette Midler at her New Year's Eve concert. Bette, clad in a diaper, introduced "Father Time." Barry, joking that she still treated him like an employee, joined her for a duet. Gone, however, was the rancor of years past. Once they had parted ways, they discovered how much they loved each other and what good friends they were. Now when they get together and he helps her musically, he does it out of love, "not because I'm her conductor," he said.

From there he headed back to the bright lights of Broadway for the second record-breaking engagement at the Uris Theatre in February of 1983. He just had time enough while he was there to donate a piano to the local High School for the Performing Arts. But the world beckoned once again. This was to be the eastern leg of the Around the World junket.

Tokyo is a magical mixture these days of young punk rockers, traditional Japanese, and innovative styles that combine the best in American and Oriental tastes. The hot neon lights of the Ginza Strip, like Times Square, advertise entertainments of all sorts. There is a great love for the West, but often the cultures clash because of simple misunderstandings about how the other operates. For Barry, stepping onto stage in front of a packed house of enthusiastic fans, there was no way of really knowing how he would be received.

Barry needn't have worried. Love, humor, and romance are universal human qualities, whatever the culture. The Japanese went wild, reissuing several of his albums on Japanese labels. The Orient is a market that Barry can count on.

Australia, too, was a new proving ground for Barry. In Sydney and elsewhere on the trip, he proved over and over that he truly speaks to the heart of people of all ages and all nations.

By October of 1983 Barry was road weary. He'd been touring since August of 1982! Even a couple of rest stops on the Riviera—where he was spotted riding in the back of a pickup truck, perched on top of his piano—made the last date a joyous relief.

A gala charity concert was arranged for the benefit of the British Fund for World Jewish Relief. Hosted by Princess Di and Prince Charles, this was an event that meant a great deal to Barry.

The concert, which saw ordinary fans rubbing elbows with the upper crust of London society, was topped off by a cruel twist of fate.

Barry turned his ankle. (That ankle . . . it has troubled him since the unfortunate date at Ebbet's Field in Denver.) It didn't stop the show, but it did make Princess Di quip, "You must get married and have someone look after you."

Barry's response was not recorded, but given the pace of his life it seems unlikely that for the foreseeable future he will have enough time to devote to any kind of relationship that demands sitting in one spot with someone else.

Changes...Again

More gold records... *Here Comes the Night* turned to precious metal after only two weeks. It was his twelfth certified hit. And it was followed in rapid-fire by another foray into the studio—which brings us to where we started, 2:00 A.M. *Paradise Cafe*.

It is a long, long road from Brooklyn. And you can bet there's a lot more road ahead.

MULTIMEDIA

BROADWAY:
LOOKS LIKE
WE MADE IT

Broadway has this magical, mystical quality.
　　—Barry Manilow, in *The New York Times*,
　　　　　　　　　　December 3, 1976

*B*arry has taken the Great White Way by storm twice in his career. The first time was in 1976 in the middle of his first major ninety-eight-city tour. The second in 1983, when as a polished veteran of the boards, he slid into town on a wave of record-breaking ticket sales.

Both engagements, at the prestigious Uris Theatre, were a test of his versatility and a testimony to his incredible ability as both a musical arranger and a showman.

Christmas In New York

December of 1976. Barry had four albums on the charts at one time, a feat equaled by only a few other singers. He had visited over forty cities in the last four months, playing to sold-out houses in large amphitheaters and stadiums. His singles, "Mandy," "Weekend in New England," "This One's for You," "Trying to Get the Feeling," and "I Write the Songs" were selling thousands and thousands of records. The album *This One's for You* sold five hundred thousand copies within *three* days of its release!

"I love my group. I love to hear myself on radio. I love the whole thing," Barry bubbled the week before he was to open at the Uris.

But the beguiling enthusiasm was only part of the story. To mount a two-week engagement at one of Broadway's largest theaters is a gigantic undertaking.

A twenty-five-piece orchestra was set to accompany Barry. The charts, arrangements, rehearsals were demanding. "New York's gonna be a killer for sure," Barry said in anticipation of the opening. "All my friends from school," he said, "were expected to be in the first night audience." This was where he had to face all the people whose opinions most mattered to him. The judgments of his hometown were all-important.

Linda Allen, who was his companion and a source of comfort and security during these trying times, offered Barry the reassurance he needed. His family also rallied around. After the endless stream of strange hotel rooms and crowded airports, there was a sense of peace.

"I've been on the road since August," he said wearily. "Now I get to go to work every night and then come home like a real person."

Home was still the apartment on East Twenty-seventh Street. Although he had the money to move to posher digs, he didn't have the time. It wouldn't be until the next year that he rented an apartment with more than one room!

Opening night was a time for frayed nerves and complete cool. Barry, after hassling over every last detail, emerged as a polished pro.

The first set featured Barry, dressed in jeans, sitting at the piano. The warmth of the show reached each member of the audience. "Once it gets underway it's a relatively simple one man show and I sing everything I know and it looks great and it's fun," he has said about his shows. "I try to sing to one person."

"You could feel what he felt. His happiness and his nervousness," remembers a member of the opening-night audience.

"I really feel like I'm home," he told the packed house during the first half, and they responded enthusiastically. Reviewers perched in prime aisle seats knew that the show was a major event. The second half would only confirm it.

Returning in gray tails and a white tie, Barry sat down at the grand piano and began to play Chopin's Prelude in C Minor. Artfully he segued into "Could It Be Magic," and it certainly was!

Even Lady Flash had their turn as they took center

stage. Reparata, Monica Burruss, and Debra Byrd were not so much an interruption as an integral part of the show, complementing Barry's intense personal style with soulful energy.

All in all the show lasted one hundred minutes and offered twenty songs that transported the audience from moments of calm reflection into laughter and flat-out born-to-boogie ecstasy.

Barry needn't have worried about the tough judgments of his hometown crowd. They loved him.

For twelve nights he played to a sold-out house. Broadway had not seen a one-man show with so much power. They honored him with a prestigious Tony Award for the mastery he displayed in this new arena.

Honors were pouring in from all over. *Record World* named him the number-one pop singer. *After Dark* magazine heralded him as the Performer of the Year. *Photoplay* and the American Music Awards would follow with citations for the favorite pop vocalist and top male vocalist of the year.

The Uris show was captured on a live album that was released in spring of 1977. It rocketed to the top of the charts in weeks.

There didn't seem to be any topping himself now. But of course he did.

Return Engagement

The years and the towns and the awards would sweep by during the next seven years, but the special feeling that Barry had for the Broadway stage never dimmed. In February of 1983 he returned to the Uris one more time. The results were astounding enough to get him into the Guinness Book of World Records. He had sold $782,160 worth of tickets in one day! That broke all records.

February 21, 1983, was opening night. Barry was in the middle of his Around the World in Eighty Dates tour. He and his crew had been putting on a very elaborate show in every locale. But for Broadway they had to add a little extra. The results were shocking, even to Barry.

"There is no way I can make money on this Uris appearance," he commented. Production costs for two weeks would add up to a staggering one million dollars.

"It didn't seem like I was doing anything extravagant," he said seriously. Having gotten used to toting around forty tons of equipment, a mechanical stage, an entourage of thirty or more people and flying in your own plane, you can forget what seems grand to the rest of the world.

The truth is that for many big stars who can play their choice of "room," the money isn't the motivation.

"I wanted a legitimate Broadway theatre, It's fun. On Broadway conditions are perfect for what I'm doing: the sound, the lights, the orchestra, the audience in the right place instead of god-knows-where in some bleachers. For a performer Broadway is a dream come true."

The show went on to a house packed with fans and the glitziest of celebs. From all over, Hollywood, Palm Springs, New York, and hideaways of the rich and famous, people poured into the Uris.

They were amply rewarded.

The audiences were made up of simple hometown folks,

too. Barry remembers fondly that a member of the audience shouted out, "Hey, Barry, an autograph for my grandfather!"

The show pulled out all the stops. Using the same staging and choreography that he had perfected on the first leg of his around-the-world tour, he swooped onto the stage in a vast array of garish, glorious costumes. Everything Barry does is touched by a blend of self-mockery and overconfidence, of the hesitant kid from Brooklyn and the flash of superstardom.

For the now-famous Copacabana number, he sprang onto the stage in a costume that was an explosion of sequins and ruffles. Huge oversized flounces of fabric adorned his arms. His chest was bared to the waist. Sewn into the costume was a thick mat of curly black hair—the manly-Manilow look combined with a fop's costume. But does he let the parody rest there? No way. Halfway through the number, to the delighted shrieks of his supposedly jaded New York audience, he pulled off the fake "rug" to reveal the real Barry. His thin, hairless, unmuscular torso fairly drowned beneath the costume.

The fans loved it. Barry's self-parody reflected his obvious joy and his pride. The song's infectious beat got everyone's feet stomping.

Without a hitch he then changed tempos and rushed headlong into a flat-out rock 'n' roll segment. He had recovered from the controversy that surrounded his release of "Oh, Julie." It was clear even his most ballad-loving fans now adored the jitterbug with Barry.

There were swing tunes, Latin sambas, and touches

of every type of music from the past thirty years filling the night.

But the core of the evening, as with all Manilow performances, was his enormously arranged, dramatic love ballads. His seven-piece band and four backup singers, who are part of his permanent touring entourage, were joined by twenty-one strings. The tears fairly dripped off each note. He did the old favorites. "A good love song never goes out of style," he purred from center stage. His closing number was a medley of his hits such as "Mandy" and "I Write the Songs."

It's hard to believe that he still felt that "I am not fashionable to like." The world was yelling for more. And so that night at the Uris, he did an encore. Just a little number with a forty-piece choir.

After the opening show, Barry's friends and business associates arranged a big party at one of New York's top nightclubs, the Red Parrot. There they lavished Barry with food, music, and people. They even went so far as to re-create Barry's backstage dressing room at the Uris.

Morgan Fairchild danced frequently with Barry that night, as did many other celebrities. Barry was in top form.

Only one more dream remains to be realized on the Broadway stage. Although Barry has commitments for more than a year ahead of time, he has claimed he'd find a way to shuffle them all, in a split second, if someone would offer him a part in a Broadway musical. In the meantime, he is constantly on the lookout for a good story line for which he can compose the music and songs. One way or the other, sooner or later, Barry will probably realize this dream, too. He has achieved record-breaking stardom in every new field he has ever entered. There is no reason to think he'll stop succeeding now.

THE TV
SPECIALS:

READY TO TAKE A CHANCE AGAIN

Television keeps its eyes open for stars on the rise. By 1976 ABC had picked Barry as a star who would sustain. They signed him to a five-year, multimillion-dollar TV deal.

The chief executive at ABC in 1976 was Freddie Silverman, the legendary hit maker and network genius who was well known for his big deals and vision. (He would eventually slide from grace, but that had yet to happen when he and Barry met to sign the deal.)

"Ten years ago I delivered mail at CBS. One of the executives I took mail to was Fred Silverman. Now he's the head man at ABC. When I went to sign the contract at ABC, he remembered me!"

"Where's the mail?" he quipped.

The mail indeed. The only mail Barry delivered to ABC

was fan mail, by the bagful, as a result of his TV specials.

The Barry Manilow Special that aired in March of 1977 was the product of three months of careful, painstaking work by Barry and the entire production company.

"Haste can hurt a performer," Barry explained. He knows the audience can tell if a show was slammed together between concerts. So he suspended his touring and sat down to work on the conception, execution, and production of his first venture into tube land.

Overexposure can also hurt a singer. For that reason he refused the offer to star in a weekly variety show for the network. He was not willing to be part of a show over which he had little control. He didn't want to end up performing songs and having guests that were chosen only to fill the time slot. He is a consummate craftsman and a determined perfectionist.

The special was spectacular. He tried to give the audience a sense of his offstage personality even though the show was set in a concertlike situation. He joked, played his favorite tunes on the piano, and kept the production as real as possible.

The results? Thirty-eight million viewers tuned in to Barry, and he was awarded an Emmy for the effort.

You would think that that kind of acclaim would satisfy him. But one year later, when he again interrupted his touring to create his second special, he turned his first success into a mere learning experience.

"The key to success on TV," he explained to *TV Guide*, "is to give the viewers a sense of the real person who comes into your living room."

He considered the first special no more than an edited

version of a Barry Manilow concert. The viewer, he felt, never got a chance to really know him as a person.

That nagging sense of failed communication tugged at the back of his mind all through the next year. The solution came to the fore one evening when he and Linda were watching TV at home.

The famous director George Shaffer of "The Hallmark Hall of Fame" and "Playhouse 90" was directing *Our Town* for TV. The intimate, personal, one-on-one impact of that show was precisely what Barry was looking for in his musical variety show.

People told him he was nuts. You can't get a dramatic director for your show. But, of course, they were wrong.

Even Shaffer was reluctant to talk about the idea at first. It seemed too outlandish. But one afternoon's conversation convinced him that Barry was sincere and furthermore that he had a really good idea.

They began a four-month collaboration. In Barry's words, "It's very difficult to do what we did. It can't be done unless *other* people want to devote four months of their lives, 24 hours a day, find the best people they can, throw out 200 ideas and go over budget and wind up spending a fortune. If they want to do that, sure they can put an hour like this together."

Barry got to try his hand at TV producing, writing, and acting. The bug for all three bit, and bit hard. "I'm gonna keep doing it," he declared at the time. The special was conceived to let people know who Barry really is. He and his cowriter and coproducer Ernie Chambers went straight for the truth.

The opening scene, which featured Barry's mother in

her famous cabdriver scene ("Do you know who Barry Manilow is?") was chosen because, in Chambers's words, "We . . . opened the show with the truest symbol of where Barry comes from."

The only guest was Ray Charles, whom Barry reveres.

The rest of the show featured Barry on a bare sound-stage of the Pantages Theater. "I fantasize about different ways of doing various songs and they actually come to life. There is no audience until the last ten minutes, when the theater magically fills up with a concert audience."

As he begins to realize the fantasy in his songs, he encounters Ray Charles.

"It was an honor to work with that man," Barry bubbled like a star-struck kid. "I was a little inhibited at first—singing a duet with him. I kept saying 'Pay no attention to the white kid.' But in the long run I think I held my own."

Other numbers, in which he also held his own, were grand Busby Berkeley–like scenes, filled with feathers and dancing girls.

In between, Barry spoke candidly to the camera. He was far more confident with this kind of light conversation than he had been on his first special.

"I was scared to death at the idea at first. I actually rented a camera and a video tape machine and practiced for a month before we started shooting. The first time I tried it in my den, I looked like an idiot. It's very difficult to talk to an inanimate object like it was a friend."

But Barry, working with Chambers and Shaffer, was able to convey that magical personal flavor that is uniquely his.

"It's fabulous," he said unabashedly of the special when it was finally all edited and ready for the air. "It's the best thing I ever saw in my whole life!"

The commitment to making his art reflect his taste and standards had placed rating concerns in the backseat. But now he was unsure. It seemed unlikely that they could top the chart-busting numbers of the first show. Still, in truth, he was not overly concerned.

"I'm not sure of the kind of ratings we're going to get," he said at the time. "I did it because of the art, because it is what I wanted to do. Most people do it because they want to get the ratings or make money. I did it because I wanted to put together the finest hour I could."

He nailed it one more time.

Because it was the second of the series, it didn't cause the surprise impact of the first show. People expected him to come up with a successful product. Though no Emmy followed, the ratings were as astounding as those for Barry's first special, and the critical reviews were very positive. Every time he goes out on a limb, the limb holds, and critics are forced, one more time, to concede that he really knows his business.

The third special, like the two that had preceded it, was a team effort that took months of sweat, toil, and trauma to produce. It was, however, even more of a full-blown musical extravaganza. It was time to let Barry explore yet new territory, as a dancer and a comic.

Using the same kind of self-parody for an opening that he did with his mom in the second special, Barry started the show with him terrorizing a driving instructor as an inept learner on the freeways of LA.

John Denver was his one guest star, and they both broke out of their conventional stereotypes by joining up to sing a series of Everly Brothers hits.

The rest of the time Barry indulged his wildest fantasies as a slick dancer and matinee idol.

Watch out, Fred Astaire! Barry gave it his all, and even his less-than-perfect dancing was charming. In a colorful fantasy number he appeared in front of a stage filled with staircases. Thirty dancers moved to the beat on the top steps.

Parodying Ginger Rogers and Fred Astaire numbers, he swooped down a long rope to "get the girl" and thrill his audience.

"It's time consuming and exhausting," he reflected after the show was recorded. "I'm in on the production ground floor.

"I'm very careful with the style and the material. I've got to be very careful because I'm involved in every facet of my life and my name goes on the final product."

May 20, 1979, was the air date of the third Barry Manilow special. It marked the end of four months of back-breaking work on the special and a wave of success that threatened to overwhelm him.

Well aware that pacing is very important for maintaining artistic output, he scheduled a three-months' break in Palm Springs after the special was completed to plan his next move.

Among the pools, and white tennis togs, the smooth social scene, and the casual monied elegance, Barry had found a retreat. As frequently as possible he dodged the Hollywood parties for those dry hills of the desert. With recording facilities close at hand, he was able to immerse himself in a life of writing and recording without distraction.

Despite the success of the ABC specials, he would not continue to produce them for that network. It was not until some time later when he signed with CBS that he began to try to make a network show again. That project, still in the debate-and-wait stages, may turn out to be a made-for-TV movie based on the song "Copacabana." In the interim he has appeared on cable TV.

His Home Box Office special grabbed so many viewers it blew the networks off the air. *Variety*, the trade paper, honored him with a front-page victory banner. His second cable TV deal, with the network Showtime, was also highly successful. The HBO special, in November of 1981, was an edited presentation of his road show at the Pittsburgh Civic Arena. The second show was a tape of his 1983 outdoor concert to forty thousand cheering English fans at Blenheim Palace.

OFFSTAGE

THE PRIVATE MANILOW

"*T*here was a sweet quality about him. He was kind of a cross between James Stewart and Ichabod Crane."

"I never met anyone who had such a natural instinct to brilliantly manage their career."

"In all the years I managed my club I never had such a difficult time with any performer as I did with Manilow."

Life in the Public Eye

Ask any three people to tell you about Barry, and you'll get three different perspectives. His impact on those who have known and worked with him is as complex as his onstage persona. Just as he is awkward and masterful, ungraceful and sexy, slick and natural when he performs, so he seems in real life.

Barry is the first to acknowledge the contradictions in his personality. But the admission does little to clear up the mystery that surrounds his private life.

"The private Barry is a quiet type," he has always maintained. "Private and quiet and grateful. I think I'm sorta in awe of what's happened to me—still."

The image that his fans have of him as a rhinestone-clad heartthrob delights and worries him. Over and over he has said he wants people to know "I am in fact a living, breathing, feeling, sensitive, gentle, man."

He knows people accuse him of getting too caught up with being a star. But he has always been aware of the perils of success. As early as 1978 he said, "The thing I'm working on most is keeping my feet on the ground in this hurricane. It is very difficult. The wind can knock you over."

On one hand Barry insists on living a "normal" life.

"I toot around in my car by myself most of the time."

"I lead as normal a life as I can, being in the public eye. It's not a big sacrifice."

On the other hand Barry hides from the public eye when offstage for fear that his fans won't like the "real" Barry. "Sometimes I don't even want to meet fans because I'm afraid I'll disappoint them." Still, Barry faces his anxiety and strives to make every record and performance as real as possible.

He communicates on a very personal level with his fans. "The audience seems to walk away," he observes, "thinking they've been in the middle of a very intimate evening, even though it's a large audience."

Still, he can be bewildered by the public perceptions of the private man.

"I don't know why anyone would think I'm a nice guy just by listening to my albums."

"I think Sinatra is a good singer," Barry said, but he can't imagine writing to him and saying "you changed my life," "you helped me get through a day," "you saved me from suicide." Yet this is what Barry gets in his fan mail. At times the power his fans invest in him seems awesome.

Still, Barry does recognize that his main appeal to his fans is the intimacy and intensity of his feelings.

"I think I'm communicating more than just the pretty notes and good lyrics. I think they're really into the human being.

"Onstage there's a whole energy trip. It's certainly a great release. I take all my frustrations of the day out in a song. Sometimes I'm not even thinking about the lyric, but of a passionate emotion—joy, frustration, anger— and it comes right out in the middle of the songs. The audience is affected by it and I feel much better after I'm done. I find I can deal with people a lot better because of it."

Onstage there is no need for privacy. Every drop of feeling is meant to be shared. That is why his fans say over and over, "He doesn't care what the critics think; he only cares about how he makes us feel."

On records, too, he strives for a sense of immediacy and humanity. As he said to the *LA Times* in 1978, "You can hear me spitting. It's emotional; it's realistic. It's the real me."

The star of stage, TV, and records knows that he communicates on a deeply personal level with his fans. And he knows that his fans number in the millions. Yet, even so, he fears, "Most of my fans would be very disappointed if they realized . . . I'm not hot stuff. I'm just a regular person. Certainly a lot of people I used to idolize weren't all I thought they were when I met them."

His desire to be known, to really talk to his fans directly, conflicts with his fears of disappointing them. He remembers his own crashing disappointments in people and doesn't want anyone to feel that way about him!

Even his mom, to whom he is very close, was a source of disillusionment for him. Once she seemed worldly and sophisticated, but when he left Brooklyn and moved into a larger sphere, she seemed no more than human. "I got angry when I first realized my mom was just another human being. I had thought she was superhuman."

Life as a superstar can make it difficult to just be yourself . . . or to maintain a firm hold on exactly who you are. As Bette discovered after the release of her second album. "When you're on the top people take it upon themselves to shoot you down." Barry, too, has been on the receiving end of some of the sharpest, most pointed criticism.

Reviewers attack everything from his voice to his nose, his walk to his lyrics.

In defense he quips, "They can't possibly insult me

more than I do myself."

As recently as November of 1984, in a review of the Radio City gig, Hank Gallo of the *Daily News* accused him of being "devoid of any visible—or audible—talent."

And that was just the opening volley.

Although the *New York Times* reviewer was slightly more generous, he still found Barry's standard fare to be "bombastic."

The *New York Post* was content to say grudgingly that "He may be the king of schmaltz, but he's also a great entertainer."

A Denver critic, however, called him a "suburban shaman" and a "one man diabetic coma plague."

So bad had the ridicule and venom of some critics become that *People* magazine, hoping to step back from the fray, awarded Manilow a mention as "Performer *People* Was Too Nasty To. Alright, you Barry Manilow fans. He's not too bad. OK. OK. What we mean is he's a stronger, more musical talent than he is often given credit for."

Barry himself concedes that he might get a little schmaltzy. "But then I see the tears on their [the audience's] faces and realize that there is something that touches them."

He has sold millions and millions and millions of records, won every conceivable award, and been cheered and mobbed by fans from Tokyo to Toronto. His all-consuming ambition keeps him out there. "I'm as dedicated as you can be. I am as committed to this job of mine and to [the fans] as I can be. I take it very seriously, and I've never, never gotten bored with the job.

"If the press and the critics want to dump on me, let
'em."

Still, the cruel edge of the press can hurt.

As a public person, he must deal not only with the
potshots of critics but with the backbiting and tensions
within the music business.

Life in the Music Business

In a business where so much money is made, where
so many people hope to coattail onto the success of others, and where no one makes it to the top without the
support and assistance of the people who work out of the
spotlight, resentments are commonplace. Anyone who
falls from a star's entourage can potentially harbor a
grudge. In Barry's career there have been lots of people
who helped him and many who are now gone from the
scene. Ron Dante, his jingles partner and producer of his
first records, no longer works with Barry. Miles Lourie,
who was his devoted manager, is now constrained by
mutual legal agreements that neither he nor Barry will
talk about each other. Others in similar positions will say
no more than the standard Hollywood hype. "Hey, I still
love him. He's a doll," gushed one superagent.

Despite the rigors of being on the road, he has never
pulled the kind of rock 'n roller stunts that have scarred
other famous music business names. Hotel rooms are not

trashed. Most of the battles come from his insistence on trying to keep things orderly. "I cannot be out of control," he claims. Unfortunately, in the crazy world of the road it takes a little disorder to get order.

BARRY:

ON HIS MUSIC, APPEARANCE, AND FUTURE

*B*arry is totally committed to the musical life. The line between Manilow the musician and Manilow the private person is blurry. But that is how it must be, for he has chosen a career that demands a blending of the two.

"I live for it," he has said of his music. It fills his leisure hours as well as his working ones.

In the ten years that he has maintained his status as a superstar, he has had to fight to find his personal space inside his career. It is an enormous machine that demands a delicate balancing act between private needs and the demands of the public.

One way to make it work, he has found, is to treat his audiences as if they were his family. He wants to feel as at home in the spotlight as he does in his den. He is delighted that "I think I could have a decent conversation with any of the people who come to hear me."

In the early years of his career, it was this concern for audience rapport that created his nervousness about center stage.

All along he had said he'd really rather be out of the limelight. It wasn't until 1977 that he finally was able to get into performing.

This growing confidence in his own choices and his obvious appeal to audiences has finally made him comfortable as a performer.

"I enjoy performing in front of a group. I didn't at first because it was terrifying but now it's a nice job. I'm having a good time...."

Choosing His Songs

He'd like to record more of his own songs on each album, but Clive Davis is highly skilled at finding songs that are perfectly suited to the Manilow style. Of all the songs he has on record, "Tryin' to Get the Feeling Again" is the only song not written (or co-written) by Barry that didn't come from Clive.

His own tunes, however, also get popular acclaim. "Copacabana," which won him a Grammy, is his song. "I'm really proud to have written that one," he said. Not only was it a commercial success, it broke new ground, hitting the disco charts as well as the Top Forty. It expanded his audience and forced the public to revise their image of him.

Other attempts at expanding his sphere, such as "Oh, Julie," were more controversial.

As early as 1978 he was trying to make peace with his fans' demands. He said, at the time, "It's just begun to sink in that the age spread I appeal to is enormous. I really did have to make some hard choices as to what would be included on the *Even Now* album, for example. As a result the album is a pretty fine combination of a lot of different tastes."

He's set very high goals for himself. "I'm trying to write standards, songs that will be around for a while." He calls his music "Permanent Wave!" "Good love songs won't ever go out of style."

On His Appearance

Barry, who is a potent sex symbol to many of his adoring female fans of all ages, has never forgotten how unattractive he felt as a child. "I have pictures that would make your hair curl," he has said.

Early on in his solo career, he was adamant about having his picture taken only from the front. In one show at New York's Bottom Line he stopped singing midsong to have the film confiscated from a photographer who had snapped his picture from the side.

But over the years he has learned that by embracing and making fun of the very qualities that others poke fun at, he makes his looks part of his appeal.

At his concert at Blenheim Palace in 1983 he had two enormous video screens behind the stage filled with pictures of his profile. Onstage he teased his fans by saying, "Men who have big noses have big (pause) hearts!"

The private airplane that he tours in has his name painted across its nose. "How appropriate," he commented wryly.

Whether he is onstage or being interviewed, over and over he turns his humor on himself. He claims to be surprised that he projects a sexy image but he knows that like other stars, such as Fred Astaire, who were not classically handsome, it is the style and "feel" that turns women on.

One fan explained it best. "What people love first about Barry is his music. Then they learn to love the man. His sex appeal is part of that love."

On His Future

As with so many aspects of his life, Barry's dreams for the future are contradictory. He is an unabashed workhorse, devoted to the real work of making music. The relentless touring, recording, promotion, and interview schedule take up forty hours a day, week after week, month after month, year after year. It is his way of life. He loves it. And it is hard to imagine that he could stop.

Yet he has said, "My goal...it's the freedom not to have to tour or give concerts if I don't want to. Right now I can't take time off to make a movie or lie in the sun. The brass ring is independence and time to enjoy your life."

Dreams of lying in the sun? That does seem relaxing.

But you'll notice he also dreams of making a movie. That's hardly taking it easy.

Movies are Barry's real dream of the future.

"I may fail as an actor but I'll fail real big. I'm not accepting any little diddly roles, *Gone With the Wind* or nothing. I intend to win an Oscar. As long as that is my obnoxious attitude then I better be ready, don't you think?"

The dream is coming into focus. CBS has signed Barry up to make a TV movie based on the song "Copacabana." There have been rumors about a movie with Frank Sinatra. Scripts come to his managers frequently, and Barry looks for scripts on his own.

To prepare for the future as an actor he continues to take lessons from the esteemed coach Nina Foch.

"... If I don't move somewhere I'll move backwards. The way I could move is to find things to learn, take risks."

LIFE AT HOME

"**I**f I'm boring, then I'm boring. I don't care."

The truth about Barry lies somewhere outside the glare of money and deals and starshine. Touring (which is a great deal of his life and business) brings out the worst in him. "Tours drive you nuts," he has said.

He is a volatile mixture of many qualities. When you think too little of yourself—"I was really ugly. I was the ugliest kid in school." When you hope for too much—"I could kick myself right now for notes I missed a year ago in Cleveland. I remember everything." When you earn more than you can ever count but still remain a poor boy from Brooklyn—"I'm playing with Monopoly money." There is a lot to deal with.

It's little wonder he feels the need to retreat from the torments of public life.

Lounging in blue jeans and a Brooklyn College sweat-shirt, Barry props his feet up in fashionable Bel Air or overlooking Central Park in Manhattan. In his luxurious homes he tries to set aside the unpleasant parts of being a superstar.

On either coast he is surrounded by musical and recording equipment that would shame most professional studios. Tape machines and mixing boards, special effects machines and synthesizers, gizmos and keyboards are part of the fun and work of making music. The walls of his homes are lined with his gold and platinum records, his awards and pictures.

In California, with a breathtaking view of the mountains to one side and lush grounds on another, he is cushioned from the world. He enjoys stargazing (instead of being gazed at himself), often using a telescope on the patio.

These days when he glances toward the heavens, he can see five stars named just for him.

The International Star Registry located in Toronto and Northfield, Illinois, has an "official" list of stars in the constellations Orion, Andromeda, Pegasus, Hercules, and Lyra. Five of these stars were selected in Barry's name by fans, friends, and disc jockeys. (For a small fee anyone can dedicate a star to someone. They don't need to be a star except in your eyes.) His certificates of registry are framed.

When he returns to New York, he can't see the stars so well. But the view from his terraced apartment lets him gaze at the city lights.

The music room and the kitchen are the most lived-in rooms. He has said that when he's home, he really likes to take it easy. "I watch television and don't shave sometimes, and don't have witty things to say.

"The days that are free I usually spend with my friends, going to scary movies, having Japanese food or playing backgammon or watching TV."

The incredible pressures he is under for most of his life make the retreat to the commonplace a joy.

He doesn't hang out with other show-business people very much, although he makes his appearances at functions that are "necessary." Melissa Manchester, Bette, Tony Orlando, his band and backup singers are among his few close friends in the business. Recently his longtime friendship with his "lady" Linda Allen appears to have faded. For years they shared homes on both coasts, travel, and companionship. But when they met with interviewers, Linda remained in the shadows. She was often described as cute and cuddly, but interviewers found out little about their commitment. Neither has commented on their apparent breakup. So now, when Barry ventures out to gala events, you never know who will be at his arm. And at home he seems content with old friends.

He visits his mom or "I just go out shopping with my two best friends from my group. I just relax by doing the ordinary things most people do."

He loves rhythm and blues records, a good book, and conversations that have nothing to do with show business.

So Barry is that splendid combination of magical star with the common touch. He is prepared to accept what the future holds. If they took his fame away from him tomorrow, he'd be sad, but he'd continue, for he hopes there is more to life than the music business and more to him than the personality that parades across the stage.

His apparent isolation from the glamorous world of show business, his maniacal drive and ambition, and his lack of time for enjoying slow-and-easy relationships may make him weary sometimes. But he's not looking to provide the press with sensational stories or tragic tales. He's having fun. So, as with many aspects of his life, he has the last word and the last laugh.

"It may make good reading that I'm unhappy, but I'm not. I'm having a fabulous time!"

APPENDIXES

TWENTY-SIX CONSECUTIVE
TOP FORTY HITS

Mandy
It's a Miracle
Could It Be Magic
I Write the Songs
Tryin' to Get the Feeling
This One's for You
Weekend in New England
Looks like We Made It
Daybreak
Can't Smile without You
Even Now
Copacabana
Somewhere in the Night
Ready to Take a Chance Again
Ships

When I Wanted You
I Don't Wanna Walk without You
I Made It through the Rain
Lonely Together
The Old Songs
Somewhere Down the Road
Let's Hang On
Oh, Julie
Memory
Some Kind of Friend
Read 'Em and Weep

WHO WROTE BARRY MANILOW'S SONGS?

Mandy—Richard Kerr and Scott English

It's a Miracle—Marty Panzer and Barry Manilow

Could It Be Magic—Adrienne Anderson and Barry Manilow

I Write the Songs—Bruce Johnston

Tryin' to Get the Feeling—David Pomeranz

This One's for You—Marty Panzer and Barry Manilow

Weekend in New England—Randy Edelman

Looks like We Made It—Will Jennings and Richard Kerr

Daybreak—Adrienne Anderson and Barry Manilow

Can't Smile without You—Chris Arnold, David Martin, Geoff Morrow

Even Now—Marty Panzer and Barry Manilow

Copacabana—Bruce Sussman, Jack Feldman, Barry Manilow

Somewhere in the Night—Will Jennings, Barry Manilow, Richard Kerr

Ready to Take a Chance Again—Norman Gimbel and Charles Fox

Ships—Ian Hunter

I Made It through the Rain—Gerard, Kenny, Shepperd, Manilow, Feldman, Sussman

Oh, Julie—Shakin' Stevens

AWARDS

Records and Albums

Barry's first 10 albums all sold at least 1,000,000 copies!

He once had 5 albums on the charts at once. Only two other artists have ever done that!

He won a Grammy in 1979 for "Copacabana."
His record sales to date surpass 50,000,000!

Stage

Special Tony Award for his first Uris Theatre appearance in 1976.

AGVA Award (American Guild of Variety Artists)—the Georgie Award two years in a row as top vocalist.

Guinness Book of World Records for selling more tickets to a Broadway show in one day ($728,160) than had ever been sold. This was for his second appearance at the Uris Theatre in 1983.

Broke Radio City Music Hall box-office records by grossing $1,886,850 in ticket sales for his 1984 appearance.

TV

Emmy Award for his first ABC special in 1977.

Ratings for HBO special broke cable TV records, rivaling network audience numbers.

Film

Academy Award nomination for singing "Ready to Take a Chance Again" for the Chevy Chase/Goldie Hawn film *Foul Play*.

Radio Airplay Awards: from BMI

Most Performed Song Award for
Could It Be Magic, 1975

It's a Miracle, 1975
Day Break, 1977
This One's for You, 1977
En El Copa (Copacabana), 1978
Even Now, 1978
I Made It through the Rain, 1981
Some Kind of Friend, 1983

DISCOGRAPHY

Barry Manilow I (1973 Arista)

Sing It
Sweetwater Jones
Cloudburst
One of These Days
Oh, My Lady
I Am Your Child
Could It Be Magic
Seven More Years
Flashy Ladies
Sweet Life

Barry Manilow II   (1974 Arista)

I Want to Be Somebody's Baby
Early Morning Strangers
Mandy
The Two of Us
Something Comin' Up
It's a Miracle
Avenue C
My Baby Loves Me
Home Again

Tryin' to Get the Feeling   (1975 Arista)

New York City Rhythm
Tryin' to Get the Feeling Again
Why Don't We Live Together
Bandstand Boogie
You're Leaving Too Soon
She's a Star
I Write the Songs
As Sure as I'm Standing Here
A Nice Boy like Me
Lay Me Down
Beautiful Music

This One's for You   (1976 Arista)

This One's for You
Daybreak
You Oughta Be Home with Me
Jump Shout Boogie
Weekend in New England
Riders to the Stars
Let Me Go
Looks like We Made It
Say the Words
All the Time
See the Show Again

Barry Manilow Live   (1977 Arista)

Riders to the Stars
Why Don't We Live Together
Looks like We Made It
New York City Rhythm
A Very Strange Medley
Jump Shout Medley
This One's for You
Beautiful Music Part I
Daybreak
Lay Me Down
Weekend in New England
Studio Musician

Beautiful Music Part II
Could It Be Magic
Mandy
It's a Miracle
It's Just Another New Year's Eve
I Write the Songs
Beautiful Music Part III

Even Now (1978 Arista)

Copacabana
Somewhere in the Night
A Linda Song
Can't Smile without You
In the Morning
Where Do I Go from Here
Even Now
I Was a Fool
Losing Touch
I Just Want to Be the One in Your Life
Starting Again
Sunrise

Barry Manilow's Greatest Hits (1978 Arista)

Mandy
New York City Rhythm

Ready to Take a Chance Again
Looks like We Made It
Daybreak
Can't Smile without You
It's a Miracle
Even Now
Bandstand Boogie
Tryin' to Get the Feeling
Could It Be Magic
Jump Shout Boogie
Weekend in New England
All the Time
This One's for You
Copacabana
Beautiful Music
I Write the Songs

One Voice   (1979 Arista)

One Voice
A Slow Dance
Rain
Ships
You Could Show Me
I Don't Want to Walk without You
Who's Been Sleeping in My Bed
Bobbie Lee
When I Wanted You
Sunday Fathers

Barry (1980 Arista)

I Made It through the Rain
Lonely Together
Bermuda Triangle
Twenty-Four Hours a Day
Dance Away
Life Will Go On
Only in Chicago
Last Duet
London
We Still Have Time

If I Should Love Again (1981 Arista)

Old Songs
Let's Hang On
If I Should Love Again
Don't Fall in Love with Me
Break Down the Door
Somewhere down the Road
No Other Love
Fools Get Lucky
I Haven't Changed the Room
Let's Take All Night

Here Comes the Night   (1982 Arista)

I Wanna Do It with You
Here Comes the Night
Memory
Let's Get on with It
Some Girls
Some Kind of Friend
I'm Gonna Sit Right Down and Write Myself a
    Letter
Getting over Losing You
Heart of Steel
Stay

Barry Manilow Live in Britain   (1982 Arista)

It's a Miracle
London
The Old Song Medley:
    Old Songs
      I Don't Wanna Walk without You
      Let's Hang On
Even Now
Stay
Beautiful Music
Bermuda Triangle
Break Down the Door
Who's Been Sleeping in My Bed
Copacabana

Could It Be Magic
Mandy
We'll Meet Again
One Voice
It's a Miracle

Oh, Julie! (extended play) (1982 Arista)

Some Kind of Friend
Oh, Julie!
I'm Gonna Sit Right Down and Write Myself a
    Letter
Heaven

Barry Manilow's Greatest Hits—Vol. 2
(1983 Arista)

Ships
Some Kind of Friend
Made It through the Rain
Read 'em and Weep
Put a Quarter in the Jukebox
Somewhere down the Road
One Voice
The Old Songs
Let's Hang On
Memory
You're Lookin' Hot Tonight

2:00 A.M. *Paradise Cafe*   (1984 Arista)

Paradise Cafe
Where Have You Gone
Say No More
Blue
When October Goes
What Am I Doin' Here
Big City Blues
When Love Is Gone
I've Never Been So Low on Love
Night Song

FAN CLUB INFORMATION

Barry Manilow International Fan Club
P.O. Box 1649
Covina, California   91722

ABOUT THE AUTHOR

Kalia Lulow is the writer of ten books including *The Freelancer's Business Book* and, as coauthor with Carole Jackson, *Color for Men*. In addition, she has scripted and written lyrics for a series of ABC-TV animated children's spots. She reluctantly admits she's been in and out of more honky-tonks and helped cart around more amps, keyboards, and mike stands than she ever thought she'd see in her whole life!

ROCK IS HERE TO STAY...
SO STAY IN TOUCH WITH THE HOTTEST ROCK STARS!

A behind-the-scenes look that is sure to please even the most well-informed fan